Living Baggage Free

A Journey To Emotional Freedom
and Healing

FAUSTA C. PHELAN

Published by Skinny Brown Dog Media
Atlanta, GA / Punta del Este, Uruguay

Cover Design by Hannah Schalles.

For Information, Contact:
Distributed by Skinny Brown Dog Media
https://www.skinnybrowndogmedia.com
Email: Info@SkinnyBrownDogMedia.com

To contact the author, visit:
https://www.fcpleadtoserve.com
Email: fausta@fcpleadtoserve.com

Library of Congress Cataloging in Publication Data
Paperback: 978-1-965235-92-8
Hardback (Dust Jacket): 978-1-965235-40-9
Case Laminate: 978-1-965235-39-3
eBook: 978-1-965235-41-6

Dedications

To my daughter Brittany Phelan, *thank you for your encouragement, your refuse-to-lose mentality, and your belief that I can do more than I give myself credit for.*

To My Siblings: Michael Phelan, Willie Phelan and Dede Phelan – *for allowing me the grace to write this story and for the beautiful reunion of our family.*

To My Friends and Greatest Influencers: *Thank you for believing in me and helping me push through.*

To My God: *To Him be the Glory.*

Table of Contents

Introduction

There are countless reasons why I decided, after so many years, to put my thoughts on paper. One of the main reasons is that I believe my story can make a difference and help someone discover their path sooner than I did in mine. This book is a journey through the stifling effects of emotional baggage and the process of overcoming it. I hope my experiences resonate with you, the reader, and help you realize that you don't have to hold yourself back any longer. Life is filled with choices, and how we choose to react to circumstances can shape the emotional baggage we carry into adulthood, our relationships, and potentially into the lives of our children.

By the time I was twelve years old, emotional baggage had already crippled my family, leaving my siblings and me with little chance to emerge unscathed. I often thanked God that I was the last born, witnessing my family's self-destruction with a determination to avoid the same fate. I wanted to survive the un-survivable with as little damage to my heart as possible. I knew that if I didn't, my future would be bleak. For years, well into adulthood, I believed that by being better than my siblings, I would achieve a better life. And to some extent, I did. But what I didn't realize was that I, too, carried my emotional baggage everywhere I went. As I grew older, the weight of my past grew heavier, and my decisions were increasingly shaped by that burden, resulting in more difficult consequences.

The irony in all of this was that I didn't think my baggage was destructive. It didn't manifest in obvious ways that would make me acknowledge the need for help. Unlike my siblings, whose rebellious behaviors were clear indicators of their struggles, my emotional baggage was hidden, subtle, and insidious. I disowned myself from them, from life, and in doing so, I believed I was protecting myself. I stayed below the radar, alone, thinking that if I didn't follow their path, I would be safe. But in truth, I wasn't living I was merely surviving.

My father once told me that by the time I was born, nobody cared. That lack of attention, while painful, may have been another blessing in disguise. It allowed me to turn out differently than my siblings. But the choices I made to survive my family came with unforeseeable baggage of their own. Initially, I believed that my baggage was the source of my strength and determination. And in some ways, it was. But as I reached my late twenties, I began to take a deeper dive into my past, and the emotional baggage I carried started to reveal itself in ways I couldn't ignore.

I began to notice patterns in my life that mirrored the very things I despised in my family. Despite my efforts to avoid the pitfalls that ensnared my siblings, I found myself making decisions based on the same unresolved issues that plagued them. I became a Christian in high school and attended a Christian college, yet I still felt out of place, just as I did with my family. The harshness and judgment of the Christian culture I encountered drove me to seek solace in more destructive environments. After all, I had survived chaos before—why not again? But this time, the stakes were higher, and the consequences more severe.

The lifestyle I adopted was short lived, but the emotional baggage lingered, waiting to rear its ugly head at every turn. I knew I wasn't living up to my full potential, but I couldn't seem to break free. At just 23 years old, I found myself with no place to live, no money, and no direction. I moved in with my aunt—an act of desperation that felt like a bitter pill to swallow. But even then, I continued to search for a way out, a way to escape the patterns that had trapped me for so long.

I fell in love, fell out of love, joined the military, got married, had a child, returned to the States, and went through several jobs and marriages. The pattern never seemed to end. I was constantly depressed, feeling like I was never getting where I truly wanted to be. Yes, I survived, and yes, I had successes. But those successes were not born from self-belief—they were fueled by a desperate need for others to believe in me, to love me, and to tell me I had value. Without those external affirmations, I couldn't achieve anything based on my own self-worth. I was in a constant state of proving myself, which meant I didn't believe I was worth anything unless someone else saw value in me first.

It wasn't until I was well into adulthood that I realized just how much my decisions in life were based on my emotional baggage. Even more importantly, it wasn't until my daughter, at thirteen years of age, that I saw myself through her eyes. She developed a love hate relationship with me—one that stemmed from seeing the baggage I carried and not liking what she saw. There was nothing more painful than recognizing my baggage in my daughter and seeing the sadness and frustration in her eyes. She hated that I didn't treat myself with respect, and I hated that she saw in me what I had tried so hard to escape.

Reconciling emotional baggage is not easy, but it is necessary. Another dark yet revealing time in my life was coming to grips with the emotional neglect and abuse I experienced as a child and how I carried that abuse into my marriages and into my daughter's life. It was during this time that I embarked on a journey to figure out who I really was, what I wanted out of life, and why I wasn't getting there. I began to ask myself hard questions: Why can't I be in a healthy relationship? Am I even capable of having a healthy, loving relationship? How can I show my daughter love or teach her how to be loved when the only love I know comes with emotional and physical bruises, manipulation, and control?

If you think these are a lot of questions, they are. The more I asked them, the deeper I fell into despair. I was tired of starting over, tired of the pattern of failure that seemed to define my life. It was time to get serious—if not for my sake, then for my daughter's. I learned that while a child's love may start unconditionally, it doesn't always stay that way. I wanted my daughter to love me unconditionally because I had never experienced that kind of love as a child or an adult. But expecting that from her placed too much pressure on her shoulders, and once again, my emotional baggage resurfaced.

This book is part of the journey of how I identified, learned, and continue to work through my emotional baggage. I cannot change the past, nor should I dwell on it, but I can forgive and make a positive emotional investment in myself. People often told me to "let go," but I never understood how. How do you let go of a past that has shaped you at the deepest level? It's a process, one that takes time, faith, acceptance, forgiveness, and self-development. I am a beautiful work in progress—there is no quick fix here. But with perseverance and self-compassion, anything is possible.

And so, the journey begins…

Chapter 1

Emotional Baggage... We all Carry it

"Cast all your anxiety on Him because He cares for you."
— *1 Peter 5:7 (NIV)*

Many times more often than I would like to admit, I found my-self staring into the sky, feeling utterly defeated, looking upward toward God, expressing my agonizing frustration. I felt like my body was too heavy to carry, but it wasn't my body; it was the baggage that made me feel like I was sinking into the ground. "God!" I cried. "God, why me? Why does this keep happening to me? Why can't I move forward? I am sick of this!" After a good cry, the breakdown finally happened. I was vulnerable, alone with myself and my God. Exhausted and emotionally drained, my only solution at that moment was to take a long, very long nap, hoping that once I woke up, I would realize that I had nothing to fear but fear itself. No matter what, I was determined to be resilient, to pick myself up, attempt to leave the baggage behind, and start all over again. Does this sound familiar? Or maybe you know someone who leans on you like this, and no matter what you offer, they still feel so defeated.

> Think about a time when you felt overwhelmed by life's challenges. What emotions were you experiencing? How did you respond to these feelings? Were you able to recognize if you were carrying emotional baggage during that time?

This is what emotional baggage looked like for me. It seemed like every situation, even the good ones, ended the same way. By the time I realized what was happening, I had once again added more weight to my baggage. I usually found myself broke, starting over, moving on to a new job, a new state, a new relationship, starting a new career, or starting something new. You name it; I was starting over. This vicious cycle was debilitating, and the longer it went on, the harder it was to leave the baggage behind. Emotional baggage was my enemy, and for a person who spent most of her childhood and adult life proving herself worthy, I was losing this battle and feeling worthless. Even worse than worthless, I was getting comfortable living in the baggage and felt very uncomfortable living in what some would say were "healthy" environments.

At this point, my life felt like a movie stuck in an endless loop. I remember the first time I became acutely aware of the baggage I was carrying. It was a moment that should have been joyous—a promotion at work. Instead of celebrating, I felt a familiar weight settling over me, whispering that I didn't deserve it, that I would fail and be exposed as the fraud I believed I was. These thoughts were not new; they had been with me for as long as I could remember, echoing the harsh words I heard growing up, the criticisms that shaped my perception of self-worth.

> **Can you identify a time when a moment of success or happiness was overshadowed by self-doubt or fear? How did your inner dialogue during that time reflect your emotional baggage?**

Thankfully, there always comes a time when you say enough is enough. The journey of healing had to begin and take hold this time. After all, I felt time and time again that I embarked on this journey before. It just wasn't sticking. Nonetheless, I was once again on a mission to understand and dig into what emotional baggage is, why it took such a toll on me, and how I could move past it. I learned that this journey, as much as I wanted it to be, is not a simple or quick fix. With continued frustration, I always found myself looking for instant results. I think that was because my focus was on surviving my baggage, not reconciling it. Thriving always took a back seat. If I was going to heal from emotional baggage, the journey must be intentional, and that requires consistency, commitment, self-discipline, and patience—all of which I needed a lot of work on.

I remember vividly the day I decided to take this journey seriously. I was sitting in my car after another failed relationship, staring blankly at the dashboard. My heart was heavy, my thoughts a chaotic swirl of self-doubt and blame. "Why does this keep happening to me?" I whispered, but deep down, I knew the answer.

I was carrying wounds that had never healed, dragging around a suitcase full of unresolved pain, fear, and shame. These emotions had become so intertwined with my identity that I couldn't separate myself from them. It was time to unpack – time to face the contents of my suitcases and deal with the pain I'd been protecting myself from for so long.

Emotional baggage can feel like a trap, constantly triggering us in ways that keep us stuck. In the Bible, John 15:5, talks about God as the vine and us as the branches, explaining that if we stay connected to Him, we'll bear good fruit. Now imagine that instead of being connected to something positive like God, we're tied to our emotional baggage. We're still branches, but the fruit we produce – our actions, our decisions, and our relationships – becomes rotten. Over time, the baggage chokes the life out of us, leaving us bearing nothing good. It's not just about missing out on growth; it's about withering away completely. That's what emotional baggage does – it steals our ability to thrive.

> What "rotten fruit" have you noticed in your life that may be a consequence of unresolved emotional baggage? How does this analogy resonate with your own experiences?

Since childhood my vine was rooted in bad soil – soil that gave me little chance to grow anything good. This set me on a lifelong search: for acceptance, for understanding, for a better way of living, for a deeper connection with God. I knew something important was buried deep inside me, but no matter how hard I searched, I couldn't reach it. This state of constant searching, followed me well into adulthood, shaping the decisions I made and the relationships I formed.

It wasn't until much later in life that I began to truly confront the emotional baggage I had been carrying since those early years. At over 50 years old, I had the opportunity to pursue a master's degree through the company I was working for, at no cost to me. I hesitated-wondering if it was worth the effort at this stage in my life. But my desire for answers and personal growth outweighed the doubt. I enrolled in a program in Executive Leadership, not realizing that this academic journey would force me to face the very thing I had been avoiding for so long: myself.

In my first class, it wasn't long before the subject of emotional baggage came up. That was the day of reckoning. Suddenly, the search I had been on for decades made sense-I was searching for relief from the emotional wounds that had been controlling me all along. It felt like an AA meeting, where you introduce yourself and confess your addiction. I could have said, "Hi, my name is Fausta, and I suffer from unreconciled emotional baggage." It became painfully clear that my unresolved emotions weren't just holding me back-they were the root cause of my poor decisions and the hurt I had caused to myself, my daughter, and those I had loved. I was finally beginning to understand the full weight of what I had been carrying all my life.

I began to look back at what it was about this unreconciled emotional baggage that affected me the most. My heart began to fill itself with sadness and despair. It was relationships and all that goes with that-love, commitment, vulnerability, patience and most of all, trust. Instead of saying to myself, "I married my father 3 times, and they were all controlling men", I took ownership and held myself accountable for my part in those failed relationships. After all, I was the common denominator in all those scenarios. That was a tough day, and the beginning of many tough days. Crying and on my knees reconciling with the past wishing I could say I am sorry but knowing that sometimes saying I am sorry brings more pain to the one you are asking forgiveness from. I just couldn't rehash an old wound for someone, just so I would feel better. I had to be sorry, let go and learn to forgive myself

Dr. Sabrina Ronanoff, a clinical psychologist and professor at Yeshiva University, refers to the term emotional baggage as unfinished emotional issues, stressors, pain, and difficulties we've experienced that continue to take up space in our minds and affect our present relationships.

This particular definition resonated with me. It was like looking in a mirror and seeing my inner child still suffering in my adult life. How could I have neglected her that way? In other words, I recognized that I had been carrying this heavy load of baggage all my life, and if I was going to move forward, this issue of emotional baggage had to be addressed. My understanding of this definition meant that my emotional baggage comprised unresolved feelings, memories, and experiences that started in my past, lived in my present, and were holding me hostage from a future I had always envisioned for myself. It was almost impossible not to agonize over this reality, but that is what emotional baggage does. It keeps you in the past. The more I dwelled over it, the heavier the load. The realization itself felt like I was adding more baggage to my already heavy load. Realization, however, doesn't always match reality. Thank God! The reality was that I had to open up the baggage— not relive it but open it up just enough so that I could release it. Yes, it was going to get emotional and sometimes too painful to bear, but anything worthwhile is always an uphill climb. Imagine carrying this baggage uphill for over 50 years! No wonder I had fallen backward and rolled to the bottom so many times. Have you ever tried to climb a hill with heavy weight? I have, literally and figuratively. It is a daunting task. If I was going to make it to the top, it was time to unload the weight.

> What unresolved feelings, memories, or experiences are you carrying that continue to affect your present life? How does acknowledging them change the way you view your current struggles?

One of the most challenging aspects of dealing with emotional baggage is recognizing it for what it is. For so long, I believed that the thoughts, the insecurities, and the fears were just part of who I was. I didn't see them as symptoms of deeper issues—unresolved pain from my past. The moment of clarity came when I realized that my reactions to certain situations were disproportionate to the events themselves. A minor criticism at work would spiral into days of self-doubt and depression. A small argument with a friend would lead to sleepless nights filled with anxiety. These were not normal reactions; they were the manifestations of emotional wounds that had never healed.

I began to understand that these wounds were like open sores, easily irritated by even the slightest touch. And just like physical wounds, they needed to be treated, cleaned out, and allowed to heal properly. But how do you treat a wound you can't see? How do you clean out years of accumulated pain, fear, and shame? The first step was acknowledgment. I had to stop running from my past and start facing it head on. This was easier said than done. The past is a scary place for those of us carrying emotional baggage. It's filled with memories we'd rather forget, decisions we regret, and people who have hurt us. But I knew that if I ever wanted to be free, I had to confront it.

I started by journaling. Every day, I would write down my thoughts, my feelings, and my memories. At first, it was just a trickle of words, hesitant and uncertain. But as the days went by, the trickle turned into a flood. I found myself pouring out years of suppressed emotions onto the page. The more I wrote, the more I began to see patterns—recurring themes of abandonment, rejection, and fear. These were the roots of my emotional baggage, the unresolved issues that had been weighing me down for so long.

But journaling was just the beginning. I knew that I needed to go deeper, to explore these issues with the help of a professional. So, I sought out therapy, something I had resisted for years. Therapy was not an easy journey. It forced me to confront parts of myself that I had buried deep inside. There were tears, there was anger, and there was pain. But there was also healing. Slowly, with the guidance of my therapist, I began to unpack my emotional baggage, one piece at a time.

> How do you currently process your emotions? Have you tried journaling or therapy? If not, what might be holding you back from exploring these avenues?

I learned that many of my issues stemmed from my childhood, from the way I was raised, and the experiences I had growing up. My parents, though I choose to believe they had their own way of showing love, were dealing with their own unresolved issues, and those issues were passed down to me. I had to come to terms with the fact that they did the best they could with the tools they had, but that didn't mean I had to carry their baggage as my own.

This understanding was both liberating and terrifying. Liberating because it meant that I had the power to change my life, to break the cycle of emotional pain that had been passed down through generations. But terrifying because it also meant that I could no longer blame my parents or anyone else for my problems. I had to take responsibility for my own healing.

The process of unpacking emotional baggage is not a linear one. It's messy and complicated, with many twists and turns along the way. There were times when I felt like giving up when the pain seemed too much to bear. But I reminded myself that this pain was a necessary part of the healing process. Just like a physical wound that hurts as it heals, my emotional wounds needed to be acknowledged and felt before they could be released.

> **What fears arise when you think about taking responsibility for your own healing? How might facing these fears empower you to move forward?**

As I continued my journey, I began to notice changes in myself. I became more self-aware, more attuned to my thoughts and feelings. I learned to recognize the triggers that would set off my emotional baggage and to respond to them in healthier ways. Instead of spiraling into self-doubt or anxiety, I would take a step back, breathe, and remind myself that these feelings were rooted in the past, not the present. This was not an easy habit to develop. It took time, patience, and a lot of practice. But slowly, I began to feel lighter, more at peace with myself and my life.

One of the most important lessons I learned during this time was the power of self-compassion. I had spent so many years being hard on myself, criticizing myself for my mistakes, and berating myself for not being good enough. But as I began to unpack my emotional baggage, I realized that this self-criticism was just another form of emotional baggage, a way of keeping myself stuck in the past. I had to learn to be kind to myself, to forgive myself for my mistakes, and to accept myself as I am, flaws and all.

This was not an easy task. Self-compassion does not come naturally to those of us who have been carrying emotional baggage for so long. But with practice, I began to change the way I spoke to myself. Instead of harsh criticism, I began to offer myself words of encouragement and support. Instead of focusing on my flaws, I began to recognize my strengths. And instead of dwelling on my mistakes, I began to focus on my successes, no matter how small they were.

> **How do you speak to yourself in moments of failure or doubt? What would it look like to replace self-criticism with self-compassion?**

As I continued to practice self-compassion, I noticed real changes within myself. I became more confident, more resilient, and at peace with who I was. The constant need for validation from others or urge to compare myself to them faded away. I felt content with where I was in life.

But even with this newfound awareness, I still had to remind myself not to be too hard on myself. While I no longer sought approval from others, the habit of self-criticism lingered. I needed to learn how to truly give myself a break.

It is easy to be hard on yourself during this journey, especially when you look back and feel disappointed for the time you think you've wasted. I've felt that way myself. However, what's more important is recognizing that this process of self-discovery and healing is an opportunity to move forward. What we learn and feel about ourselves offers the chance to unpack the emotional baggage and continue growing.

But perhaps the most profound change I've experienced so far is in my relationships. As I began to let go of my emotional baggage, I found I was able to connect with others on a deeper level. The fear of rejection and the need for approval, while still present at times, no longer held me back as much. I could begin to be more myself- authentic and even sometimes vulnerable (that is a tough one) - without as much fear of judgement or criticism. In doing so, I started to attract people into my life who accepted and loved me for who I was, even if I was still learning to fully believe in that love and acceptance myself.

This was a powerful realization for me. For so long, I had believed that I was unworthy of love and acceptance, that I had to be someone else to be loved. While I still sometimes struggle with those old beliefs, I now understand that the person I need to be is myself. And as I continue to let go of my emotional baggage, I'm learning that I can find love and acceptance by embracing who I truly am-even if it's an ongoing journey.

> **Reflect on a relationship in your life. How might your emotional baggage have influenced your interactions in that relationship? What would it mean for you to connect with others without the weight of your past?**

The journey to emotional freedom is not an easy one. It requires courage, commitment, and a willingness to face the pain of the past. But it is a journey worth taking. Because on the other side of that pain lies a life of freedom, peace, and self-acceptance. A life where you are no longer weighed down by the past but are free to live fully and authentically in the present.

As I stand here today, I am not the same person I was when I started this journey. I am stronger, more resilient, and more at peace with myself and my life. I have let go of the emotional baggage that has weighed me down for so long, and in doing so, I have discovered a life of freedom and joy that I never thought possible.

> **What steps can you take today to begin your journey toward emotional freedom? Reflect on the areas of your life where emotional baggage is most present and consider how you might start the process of unpacking and releasing it.**

As we close out this chapter on the emotional baggage that we all carry, it's essential to recognize that acknowledging this baggage is the first step toward healing. We've explored the origins of our emotional burdens and how they shape our interactions, decisions, and relationships. This understanding empowers us to make different choices—ones that are rooted in self-awareness and a commitment to growth rather than survival.

Emotional baggage may feel like a heavy burden, but remember, it's not a permanent fixture. It's a part of your past that you can choose to learn from rather than letting it define your future. The journey to emotional freedom is ongoing, and each step you take is a victory in itself.

As we move forward into the next chapter, we'll delve deeper into the origins of this baggage—where it truly begins. We'll explore how generational patterns, family dynamics, and early experiences lay the foundation for the emotional baggage we carry. Understanding these roots are crucial because it allows us to address the underlying issues at their source, giving us the power to break free from cycles that may have persisted for generations.

Prepare to journey into the depths of your past, where we'll uncover the seeds of your emotional struggles and begin the process of uprooting them. By doing so, we can pave the way for a future unburdened by the weight of unresolved issues. This next step is vital in your journey to living a life that is truly baggage free.

Chapter 2

The Roots of Emotional Baggage

"The Lord is close to the brokenhearted and saves those who are crushed in spirit."
— *Psalm 34:18 (NIV)*

The Source of Our Struggles

Well, here we are—the million-dollar question: **Where does emotional baggage come from?** We know that emotional baggage refers to unresolved emotional issues from our past that continue to occupy space in our minds. The key to this is the word *"experienced,"* which points to the fact that the root cause of emotional baggage often lies in past events.

It sounds simple, right? But is it really? The journey of uncovering the source of our emotional baggage is often a painful one.

That's why, before I could even begin to let go, I needed to first understand and reconcile the emotions that triggered my baggage in the first place. Emotional baggage can be complex, encompassing a range of emotions—fear, guilt, regret, low self-esteem, insecurity, and trust issues. I felt all of them. Sometimes all at once, sometimes at different times, and each of these emotions seemed to have layers upon layers, like peeling back an onion.

Maybe that's why it's so difficult to truly let go of emotional baggage. Just when you think you've released guilt or fear, you uncover it again, buried deeper, triggered by something completely different. This complexity can be overwhelming. Knowing this, and fearing I might never fully overcome my baggage, I had to ask myself one hard question: *Was I really ready to face it?*

It's easy to play the blame game here. We can blame our parents, extended family, society, and the friends we chose to hang out with in school, but doing so only feeds into our emotional baggage and perpetuates it. While it doesn't seem fair, the truth of the matter is life is not fair. The good news is what we choose to do with the cards we're dealt is on us, and that is what makes it fair. If only as children, we could grasp the concept of choice vs. survival sooner rather than later.

Choice vs. Survival: A Hard Truth

Choice is a wonderful thing, but no one ever said that choice was easy. My brother Willie said, "When you're very young, you don't realize you are making choices, especially damaging ones. In the end, you're just trying to find anyone or anything that will give you solace in a world that is so cruel to live in." When you're young, what does choice mean anyway? We know that something is very wrong but don't have the maturity or remedy to do anything about it. However, the older we become, the more determined we are to find a way out. Whatever it takes. Wherever it lands us. We will deal with the consequences as they happen. There it is—the cliff that so many children face and too many fall off. As the youngest of four children, I watched each of my siblings fall off this cliff headfirst. It's heartbreaking and very lonely to watch. To this day, I can't explain why I discovered "choice" before they did. Maybe, I often wonder, it's because I was the youngest, and I had what seemed to be a crystal ball of watching what my life would be like if I followed my siblings' path. Their pain, their suffering, their search for solace became my unknown opportunity of choice. That is not to say that I escaped the rapture of my family, but the choices I did make were a lot less self-destructive than theirs.

> **Is there a time when you observed others making self-destructive choices? How did witnessing their struggles influence your own decisions?**

Family Dynamics: The Seedbed of Emotional Baggage

The roots of emotional baggage can run deep because, for the Phelan kids, it was rooted in layers of family trauma. This complicates things because, like all children, we are emotionally and physically dependent on our parents. We want to be loved and feel safe. We want to be wanted, not considered a burden. Our parents, no matter what they are going through, are our heroes, even if we discover they are villains. It's the mixed messages of what they say vs. what they do that caused confusion in our hearts and minds.

I remember my mom telling me that she loved me, but the love between my parents was so volatile that when she said she loved me, I wondered if love included bullying and verbal abuse, we all took from my father. I wondered if the love she had for me included all the lies she used to tell my father to get his attention as well as to protect us from being hit. I remember I couldn't rely on my mother. It was very strange; while to the outside world it seemed as if she was very loving, caring, and would give you the shirt off her back, to the four of us kids, she was not nurturing. It was as if her children were an end to a means, trying to save her marriage. My sister and I agree we were not given the tools to grow up to be strong, successful, and emotionally healthy women. Is this the love she was talking about? As a young girl, all I saw was a woman who couldn't or wouldn't stand up to a man who degraded her. My mother was desperate, and she would stir the pot at any cost to get my dad's attention or have things her way. Is this love? The love I saw in my home was much different than what I thought love should be. Lying and deceit, regardless of the reason, became the definition of what my mom's love meant to me.

> **Reflect on how your family dynamics shaped your understanding of love and relationships. What patterns have you carried into your own life?**

My father's ability to love was completely opposite. He would only show you his approval if you met all his criteria. It was very conditional, and for him, showing love was never really an option. When you didn't meet the condition, love turned into dislike, and dislike turned into hate. As kids, we were in a constant state of proving ourselves worthy. Everything was black or white with my dad. You were either a success or a failure. There was no middle ground. If you were a failure in his eyes, you paid a huge price. You were beaten, threatened, degraded, and ultimately discarded. When kids live in that type of environment, failure is inevitable, which means we either constantly tried to please my dad to no avail, or we rebelled and lived the label he put on us—failure. My siblings for many years lived the latter. After many tries of pleasing him, they gave up, and by the time they were in their young teens, they all found themselves on that cliff, ready to jump off into a life of destruction.

Remember, all kids want is to be loved, accepted, and safe. If you are not getting that at home, you will find it somewhere, and since misery loves company, falling into a destructive path appears to be the path of least resistance.

To paint the full scope of life in the Phelan home, it is important to describe what those "choices" looked like. Michael, as we called him, was the oldest. His job was to live in my father's image. Whatever my father couldn't accomplish as a kid, my brother had to make up for. He was supposed to be the "star" of the family, but as he came into his own, he realized that the life he was commanded to live was not his. With expectations set so high, there was nowhere to go but down. One disappointment after another, Michael was no longer in my dad's good graces. The more my brother veered off, the uglier my father and he got. There were even times when father and son threatened to seriously hurt each other. As he approached junior and senior high school, he became a wise guy and bully at home, especially when my father was away—ironically, just like my dad.

However, in school, he strived to be the most popular, the class clown, and it seemed to work for him. Being the most popular guy at school replaced being unpopular at home. He was never the protector like most big brothers try to be—a regret that he lives with to this day. In fairness to him and the rest of my siblings, for that matter, we were raised not to love each other but to work against each other. After all, it was survival of the fittest. Being the center of his circle became Michael's mission. As an adult, he found his center. He maintained control by getting involved in the drug scene in Miami. There he presented himself like a king and once again he was the most popular guy, but sadly for all the wrong reasons. If only his talent of the "art of persuasion" could have been used differently.

Willie was the next in line, eighteen months younger than Michael. My father had serious issues with him. By the time my mom was pregnant with Willie, I believe my father was having an affair and wanted out of the marriage. Having a second child ruined those plans. Willie was my mom's favorite, probably because he was born out of an attempt to save her marriage. My dad, on the other hand, I believe, always resented Willie. To make matters worse, Willie struggled with academics from an early age, and this difficulty followed him throughout his education. He may not have been considered "smart" by traditional standards, but I remember vividly that even as a child he could take apart television and reassemble it perfectly, as though it had just come from the store. Back then, televisions were complex inside- more like car engines than the sleek devices we have today.

We believe he may have had a learning disability that back then wasn't recognized. When he got left back in first grade, that was the beginning of my father's disdain for him. In my father's eyes, he was stupid and useless. Willie was the recipient of the most verbal and physical abuse in the family. He was scared and desperate for love. The more my mom tried to protect him, the more my father abused him. By the time he was 13, he had vandalized a home and was using some very serious drugs. When I asked him why he made that "choice," he said, "It wasn't a choice per se. I felt safe and accepted with the crowd of kids that probably felt the same way, and the drugs took away my fear." Willie's story of recovery and healing is nothing short of amazing, and I am incredibly proud of him. I'm deeply grateful that he's still here to share his journey, and his resilience has become a source of inspiration for many others who have walked a similar path.

Then there was my sister Dede, eighteen months younger than Willie. Dede had a simple soul and just wanted to be loved and belong. She had such an innocence to her, which made it very easy for my father to manipulate her self-worth. The one thing a little girl wants is her father's love. Instead of love, my father gave her constant ridicule. I distinctly remember three things about my sister when she was young. First and foremost, she wanted to be a nun. Her favorite movie at that time was *The Bells of St. Mary*. She just loved the idea of serving and helping others. The second thing I remember is that she ate very slowly. So slowly that my father would take her food and dump it on her because he couldn't stand watching her play with her food. So many times, spaghetti would be on the wall because my father would throw it on her or dump it on her. Finally, I remember that in my father's eyes, Dede was very dumb. He made up a song that further instilled her belief that she was dumb. The song was called "Dede Dumb." My father sang it all the time—so much so that when she would get into arguments with us, we all sang the song at one time or another.

As Dede was approaching her teen years, she caught a break and found common ground with my Dad. It gave us all hope, but it was short lived. By this time, my dad owned a horse and played polo. Dede loved horses and learned to be a good rider, which earned the approval from my Dad we all yearned for. She would spend a lot of time at the barn with my father, walking his horse and getting involved. They had a connection until the one fateful moment when Dede went to the barn and my father told her she was no longer allowed to go there. He was having an affair and filing for divorce. Nothing would ever be the same. Dede was devastated and abandoned in front of all the folks at the barn. My father exiling her was the "cliff" she was on. She was drinking, doing drugs, cutting school, and hanging out with some of the toughest girls I have ever met. Her "choices" drove a huge stake between us. It was hard enough being her sister; now I began to really despise her. We constantly fought, and she would always win. I was petrified of her and her friends.

Sadly, Dede and Willie were eventually worn down. When someone you love consistently beats your self-worth down you start to believe them, which is exactly what happened to them. They were brainwashed by the words of my father, "You are not smart and will never amount to anything." Both of them dropped out of high school in 11th grade. Like Willie and Michael, Dede found her safe place in drugs and reckless living. By the time she was 19, she was married to a roadie of a rock band. She finally belonged and found her way out, or so she hoped. It was hard for me to watch my siblings self-destruct, one at a time. I felt like I was living outside a circle with no door inviting me in. I think some part of me wanted to be rebellious because maybe then I could fit in. Have you ever felt like an outsider in your own family?

Usually, family is what you turn to, but in my case, family was my stranger. The more the vicious cycle kept going, the more abandoned I felt. Abandonment for me was not defined in the traditional sense of physical abandonment. Up until my parents divorced, no one left physically, however, it was emotional abandonment, one that stayed with me for what seemed like forever.

As for me, I don't have the memories that my siblings have, but I have enough to know that dysfunctional marriages are brutal for children. There were some things that occurred in my family that I would not wish on anyone, especially once my father finally decided to go through with divorcing my mom. For me, that period of time was the most violent and emotionally abusive time of my life. However, when I was very young and maybe too young to remember, I believe to keep my sanity, I subconsciously blocked a lot out. My brother and some of my relatives tell me I was very neglected. I would be in the crib for hours at a time with dirty diapers. No one ever played with or took care of me unless it was a last resort. I was the outcast, another unwanted child and my mom's last-ditch effort to keep my dad from leaving her. By the time I was born, no one had the energy to care, so I felt, why bother caring myself, especially for me?

One of the things I do remember about myself is something that most would be embarrassed by – trust me, I am – but allowing myself to be vulnerable here is the only way I know how to tell my story. Someone out there has likely gone through the same thing, and the hope of healing is worth the embarrassment. When I was very young, I used to hate taking a bath, brushing my teeth, or combing my hair. I guess, looking back, I shouldn't be so surprised since I sat in a dirty diaper for hours. It was like pulling teeth to get me to do these things that meant taking care of myself. When forced to, I would sit in the bathroom for about an hour, filling up the tub and never going in it. I would dip my head in just enough to get it wet and swoosh the water around, so everyone thought I was taking a bath. My father knew what I was doing, but all he had to say was, "Let her rot!" I think as young as I was, it was my way of getting my family to pay attention to me. Thankfully, I grew out of it, but it lasted a long time, and I did get that attention I was yearning for, but it wasn't in a way that was helpful. I became known as the ugly duckling, not only in my immediate family but in my extended family as well. Long after I outgrew the hygiene issue, my father would say I was ugly. My mom, on the other hand, would say I was attractive, which meant to her, I looked good from far away, but up close, not so much. Being ugly became what I was known for throughout the rest of my school years; at least that is the way it felt for me. I had bucked teeth and a head that was much bigger than my body. I didn't wear makeup like my sister, and I loved dressing like a tomboy. The dirtier the better. I even dressed like I was ugly. My sister was the pretty one, and I was constantly reminded of that, which made me feel even more isolated and neglected. Like the rest of my siblings, I took my share of beatings, but not nearly as much as them. Being the youngest afforded me the opportunity to observe and retreat before getting on my dad's bad side.

A Defining Moment

One of those harsh truths came crashing down at the dinner table. I will never forget the day it was my turn at the dinner table to be called a failure, to be told I wouldn't amount to anything. My father's words were sharp, like they had been with my siblings and much like their story, my mother just sat there and said nothing. She was as afraid as we were. This time, however, the results were going to be different. Inside, I was defiant. "NO WAY! I am not going down that path-come hell or high water!" But in front my father, at the dinner table, all I could manage was, "No Dad, I promise." His response, "Don't count on it, see these three dummies." It was before my parents' divorce so I must have been 11 or 12 years old. By the grace of a God I didn't know at the time, I made a vow that day: I would not, under any circumstances, even if I have to hate my siblings, I was not going to follow in their footsteps.

Coping Through Dance

My coping rested in my imagination. When no one was around, I would move all the furniture in the living room and dance to Tchaikovsky's War of 1812. This powerful music helped me rid myself of fear, filling me with strength and confidence. With this music, I imagined that I was performing the greatest dance routine next to the orchestra. I was barely 4'feet tall but I felt like I was a giant when I danced to this music. Each movement freed me from the weight of my family's dysfunction. When I danced, I was unstoppable. I was magnificent. You could see it in every move I made.

There was another song that I used to dance to more often than Tchaikovsky's War of 1812. It was a song of pure emotion. It was as if I wrote the song. It reached deep into my soul and allowed me to cry out my loneliness and desperation. When I was done with this song, I dropped to the floor, emotionally and physically exhausted looking up to a God that I had no understanding of and wasn't sure existed. God didn't matter to me then. Whatever was up in the sky, I was singing with tears and dancing with all the muster and feelings I had. The show was called *A Chorus Line*, directed by Michael Bennett, 1975. The song, *Music in the Mirror*, music by Marvin Hemlish, lyrics by Edward Kleban. It was the first Broadway show I had ever seen and to this day the one that still reaches deep into my soul. The scene was about a woman who had experiences greatness on Broadway, but now she was washed up. Too old for what the Director wanted and, on her way, out of the business, fighting to stay in, to be a part of something she loved so much. Watching this scene was like looking at myself in the mirror, only in 1975 I was just 14 years old, feeling washed up and no longer belonging to anything. My life would have no purpose if I couldn't fit it. These lyrics owned me. I remember dancing as if I was begging, pleading with someone to love me, hear me and bring me closer. There was a mirror in my living room and like the character, Cassie, I sang into it as if it was my father, not the director, and begged that he would give me a chance to show him what I had and then I danced. I danced my heart out, hoping he would say, "You did good, I got you."

The Music in the Mirror
Give me somebody to dance for,
Give me somebody to show.
Let me wake up in the morning to find
I have somewhere exciting to go.

To have something that I can believe in.
To have something to be.
Use me... Choose me.

God, I'm a dancer,
A dancer dances!

Give me somebody to dance with.
Give me a place to fit in.
Help me return to the world of the living
By showing me how to begin.

Play the music.
Give me the chance to come through.
All I ever needed was the music, and the mirror,
And the chance to dance for you.

Give me a job and you instantly get me involved.
If you give me a job,
Then the rest of the crap will get solved.
Put me to work,
You would think that by now I'm allowed.
I'll do you proud.

Throw me a rope to grab on to.
Help me to prove that I'm strong.
Give me the chance to look forward to sayin':
"Hey. listen, they're playing my song."

Play me the music.
Give me the chance to come through.
All I ever needed was the music, and the mirror,
And the chance to dance...

Play me the music,
Play me the music,
Play me the music.
Give me the chance to come through.
All I ever needed was the music, and the mirror,
And the chance to dance...

It wasn't until much later in life that my father finally admitted to me, he had no interest in loving me or investing in me. He saw what had become of his other children, so why bother with me? It was no wonder why I felt alone and did not belong to anyone. My love for dance and the escape it provided gave me a safe place as well as a place where I wasn't going to follow in the footsteps of my siblings.

Not only was I alone, but as I began to experience "loving" relationships, I became like my dad; I could take them or leave them. It is sad, but I think all the kids inherited the ability to just cut people out of our lives. One minute I would find myself in love, and then, without realizing when it happened, I was out of love. It's as if my ability to love never had the capability of running deep. Maybe it was the coping skill of keeping my emotional distance so as not to get hurt. Eventually, that coping skill becomes emotional baggage that holds me back from truly being able to love someone.

1 Corinthians 13, the well-known chapter in the Bible that speaks about love, is a type of love I would dream about but never quite got it. I just felt incapable of being able to feel like that.

1 Corinthians 13

Love is patient; love is kind. It does not envy, it does not boast,
it is not proud.
It does not dishonor others, it is not self-seeking, it is not easily
angered, it keeps no record of wrongs.
Love does not delight in evil but rejoices with the truth.
It always protects, always trusts, always hopes, always perseveres.
Love never fails.

Love as defined by me living in my childhood home:

Love was shown as having no patience.
Love was never kind; instead, it was ugly, mean, and physically
and emotionally damaging. Love does boast and is defined by
narcissism.
It continually dishonored others, was very self-serving, and was
very easily angered and consistently kept records of wrongs.
Love delighted in pain, evil, and punishment.
Love was a lie, a misconception of what it means to care for
someone.
Love never protected me.
I could never trust it, and my only hope was that someone would
find me and take me away. Love never lasts, and it had always
failed me.

As my father would say, "With a love like this, who needs en-
emies." He was right; I was living in what felt like enemy territory.
I think as I grew older, I strived for a love like 1 Corinthians 13
but ended up with a hybrid between the "love" I grew up with and
love as God describes it. This struggle of understanding love would

eventually lead me to several destructive relationships, divorces and a whole lot of unreconciled baggage.

We were just little kids then. What did we know? Today, when asking my siblings what drove you to the cliff? What were the emotions that drove you to make the unconscious choices you made? All of them had the same answer: We felt scared, insecure, and just wanted to feel like we were worthy of love. We just wanted to be accepted and belong. Being loved by my dad meant that we all had to earn it. Wasn't love within a family supposed to be unconditional? How can it be when we all live in a house filled with emotional baggage we did not ask for, yet still suffer the consequences? To this day, I always tell my daughter, "Don't carry someone else's baggage on your shoulders. It only makes the load heavier when you're already carrying your own.

The Burden of Generational Baggage

The advice I gave my daughter became very real to me as a child. There was one very distinct day I realized, how could my father love any of us if he didn't love himself? My dad was a blue-collar worker and had been laid off from the union for a couple of months. I will never forget the day I saw my dad staring out the living room picture window. He did this a lot, but this time something was different. It was sometime in the mid-1970s. He stopped and stared out the window in the bold stance that he was famous for. His face was broken. He looked so defeated, like life really screwed him, and he was stuck and couldn't get out. There was a tear in his eyes, which for me was an unrecognizable sight. My dad didn't cry. The man that I was trying so hard to please was broken. He looked very unloved himself. How can he love me if he doesn't love himself? Did he ever love me? How can I love him more so that he can love me in return? All those questions ran through my mind. At that moment, I knew his anger toward his family was a direct result of the anger he had within himself. He obviously didn't want to be there, and eventually, he found his way out—his place where he felt like he belonged. Her name was Marie, and while she wasn't my mother, ironically, she was the best thing that ever happened to my dad. In her heart, she wanted to heal him and help reconnect him with his children, but that only happened for me. When Marie died, the Phelan kids were with him, showing our support and pouring love on him, but the anger he had toward my siblings ran too deep-a wound even Marie couldn't heal. Eventually my dad married again but our relationship went from healed to very distant. Without Marie, he went back to his old self.

If we stop right here, it would be understandable why children often get caught up in the blame game as to why their lives suffer as adults. "It was because of my family." "Growing up in my family, I didn't have a chance in hell of making it!" "Of course, I am a failure; that is what I was raised to be." "No one ever loved me, so why should I love myself?" If you have ever found yourself saying these things, then this is your opportunity to address your emotional baggage. If you are thinking these types of thoughts, then you are ready to learn the life changing choice of knowing that just because I was raised this way doesn't mean I have to stay this way. This is the beginning of compassion, not blame.

Compassion and Understanding: Breaking the Chain

Compassion and curiosity led me to what I will refer to as generational baggage. This is emotional baggage that has been unresolved from generation to generation. Very simply put, when we don't resolve our emotional baggage before we decide to get married and have children, chances are your children will pick up the same baggage and carry it in their lives. In my experience, I have noticed that the consequences of that baggage are far worse as it passes through generations. The apple doesn't fall far from the tree, but if you are not careful, it can become rotten.

The weight of being a positive role model for your family is very important and shouldn't be carried lightly. However, the weight becomes heavier when parents carry the struggles they experienced growing up into their adult lives. Just like my emotional baggage was rooted in my early years of childhood, so was theirs. After all, parents were once children, vulnerable like I was, vulnerable like my siblings were. If I could figure this out, then I would replace blame with compassion and understanding. Then I can also stop blaming myself and accept things as they are, recognizing that they too lived in a place of agony. Now, this does not mean that what has happened is justifiable. It means that forgiveness can happen when compassion exists.

> **How can you replace blame with compassion in your own life? Reflect on how this shift in perspective could change your relationships.**

How could two people be so damaging to their children? No one grows up in life and says, "I want to create a destructive and volatile environment for my family." What was it about my parents that was so combustible? Why was my dad a totally different man with his second wife than with my mother? What made my dad such an angry human being? Why couldn't my mom ever get over the divorce? Why didn't she want more for herself? Why did she always seem so desperate to be the center of attention? So many questions. It was time to find the answers. After all, my sister and I had children, and our baggage was now sitting on their laps. I had to be better. I had to show my daughter that I can be different, and she didn't have to carry the same emotional baggage that I had carried. Unfortunately, hiding my baggage didn't make it hard for her to find. She was 16 when she blew up and screamed in desperation to get my attention. She saw me as weak, the same way I saw my mom as weak. She saw me being treated with no respect, like how my dad treated my mom. She saw me put men before her, much like my mom chose to put my dad over her kids. I thought I was doing everything right. I taught her to be strong, even when I wasn't, and it was that strength that she used to confront me. Her biggest fear was that she needed a mom who could be a good example for her. She needed to lean on me, and I wasn't nurturing. Some of the damage had already been done, but doing nothing was not an option. It was a devastating time of my life when my daughter confronted me with all this. That moment of realization I what started my journey.

Amidst my crying, I was deeply angry with myself. It was a failure far greater than I had ever experienced. I was in a state of shock. How could I have been so wrong? How could everything that I thought I was doing right be so wrong? Was it even fixable? I thought I ruined my daughter forever. I can't undo what was done, but I needed to make some changes. The woman she believed I could be was in there deep inside me. I just needed to learn how to let her out.

That dreadful day that my daughter confronted me was the day I realized that emotional baggage travels from one generation to another. Now, at the time, I couldn't identify it as such, but I knew enough to realize that I inherited some of the negative traits, the traits I swore I would not be like, of both my parents. My first step was to take myself out of the equation and address all the questions I had regarding my parents. Before I could get to the questions above, I had to first address the most important question—Who are they, and what created their baggage?

Understanding My Parents: The Root of the Cycle

First stop—Mom:

Born in Puerto Rico in very poor circumstances, my mom was the oldest of seven children. However, by the time she was 3, there were just 4 kids. To relieve the financial burden that my grandparents were under, they made the decision to have my mom raised by a couple who were in a better position to provide my mom with a better life. Essentially, she was given away. I don't want to even imagine what that handover must have felt like to my mom. At 3 years old, you don't know what is happening. You just cry like most 3-year-olds do when they are separated from their parents, even if it is just for a few hours. Do you think she felt like she belonged? As a result, it didn't take long for her siblings not to like her When visiting her biological family, she became difficult to be around. She was spoiled, living the life of an only child, and would not share her toys. However, unknowingly, that young girl was starving for her family's attention. She loved her family and may have felt a huge sense of rejection, which may have led to her distortion of love—doing whatever it takes to be loved, even if it meant lying and being deceitful. By the time my mother was 7 or 8, my grandparents had 3 more children but never brought my mother back home. What? Yes! She stayed with Momita Faustita and Popito William until she was 16 years old when she went to college in NYC. During this same time, her biological family moved to Long Island, NY, but hung around different circles. After all, my mom went to college in NYC, and her siblings didn't. Ironically, all this opportunity couldn't replace the emotional baggage of abandonment that she carried until her death.

Second stop—Dad:

My father was an only child, and just as his children couldn't ever please him, he could never please his parents. He was an isolated boy who was shot down many times for his dreams of being a cowboy or race car driver. My grandmother raised him with an iron fist. Nothing less than perfection was demanded of him. She wanted my dad to be what my grandfather wasn't. She held my father to a very high standard and always made sure he was dressed well, better than any other kid in school, which resulted in him being a loner. He was very smart—borderline genius by some standards—but never wanted to go to college. I think he really resented my grandmother's iron fist approach. His life was full of regret, never achieving what he was capable of, all to send a message to his mother that he would not be controlled. My father was caught between a rock and a hard place. He hated that his father was an alcoholic, gambler, and womanizer, but eventually he picked up the womanizer habit. He hated that my grandfather protected my grandmother while at the same time always cheated on her. My dad did not have addictions, but he did make a point to be the life of the party or make sure everyone feared him. That was his source of control.

All in all, the root cause of my siblings' and my emotional baggage was generational trauma, compounded by some pretty traumatic events. The irony of how similar my parents' baggage was is mind-blowing. Both of their fathers were alcoholics and disloyal to their wives. Both of their mothers believed that was just the way things should be and were married to very controlling men who used their children to make up for it.

It didn't stop there. Remember, my mom was the oldest of seven kids. All the women in my mother's family married alcoholic and/or abusive or controlling men, which in turn meant my cousins and I, who were girls, followed the same path. My mother's brothers—two of the three—were alcoholics, but all three of them married women who were strong and somewhat controlling. And finally, the children of all these people. Let me just say this: multiple marriages for most of us, lots of addiction issues, and tremendous heartbreak in the family chain.

This is the destruction of generational emotional baggage. This is what we, if we become aware, need to grab hold of and do our best to break the chains that we have been welded to by birth. It is never too late. Do we really want our children to pass this on to theirs? Are you one of those children? Know that healing can take place no matter your age. As for my siblings and me, it took many years—years we can't get back, but also shouldn't look anymore. We have reconnected. Our love for each other is being built on a firm ground of respect for each other's journey. The blame game is over.

> **Consider the generational patterns in your family. How have these patterns influenced your behavior and beliefs?**

Choosing Compassion: The Power of Perspective

After a lot of reconciling, I learned that choice must be made earlier in life. The choice you have, at the very least, to change your mindset from victim to victor is yours despite the situation you are living in. Is it easy? No, choosing your mindset can be much more challenging than physically getting out or rebelling against the horrible situation you are in, but it is a fight worth fighting for. Emotional baggage can only be overcome by who you are from the inside out. It is the choice of mindset that makes all the difference in how you survive the baggage of your past. We weren't promised a rose garden, but it doesn't mean that we must settle for the thorns.

> But there's one thing I want you to know
> You better look before you leap,
> still waters run deep,
> and there won't always be someone there to pull you out.
> And you know what I'm talking about.
> I beg your pardon,
> I never promised you a rose garden.
> Along with the sunshine,
> there's got'ta be a little rain sometime.
> I beg your pardon,
> I never promised you a rose garden.
> —Lyrics from "Rose Garden" by Lynn Anderson

As we come to the close of this chapter, it's clear that the roots of emotional baggage run deep, often entangled with the complexities of our family dynamics, societal influences, and generational patterns. The choices we make—consciously or unconsciously—are shaped by the unresolved emotions we carry from our past. Breaking free from the cycle of pain and hurt that has been passed down through generations begins with recognizing these patterns. It's not an easy journey, but it's a necessary one if we wish to live a life free from the burdens of our past.

The reflections and insights shared in this chapter are not just stories of struggle but also of survival and the potential for growth. As we move forward, the focus will shift from understanding where this baggage comes from to identifying it within ourselves. Only by recognizing the specific forms our emotional baggage takes can we begin to dismantle it and prevent it from shaping our future.

In the next chapter, we will dive deeper into the process of identifying the baggage we carry. It's one thing to understand the origins of our pain but another to see how it manifests in our daily lives and decisions. Together, we'll explore practical steps to confront and address these deeply rooted issues, empowering you to reclaim control over your life. Let's continue this journey with an open heart and a commitment to healing, knowing that identifying our baggage is the crucial step towards lasting change.

Chapter 3

Identifying Your Baggage

"Cast light and people will find the way"
— Ella Baker

Now that we've explored the concept of emotional baggage, it's important to take a closer look at the specific emotions that often come with it—fear, insecurity, anxiety, and issues surrounding self-worth, to name a few. These emotions are usually tied to past experiences and can turn into unresolved baggage that weighs us down. At the heart of this emotional burden are events or experiences that share a common trait: they remain unresolved. Without resolution or closure, these emotions continue to fuel a cycle that leads us to the same emotional destination over and over again. It's like being stuck on a train with no idea how to get off.

Emotional baggage can often be understood as a cause-and-effect relationship. The *cause* is what happens to us, and the *effect* is the emotional response we develop as a result. For instance, growing up in a violent household where I was neglected or abandoned (the cause) led to my deep-seated fear of failure and feelings of insecurity (the effect). Another example might be someone who has been consistently lied to or abandoned in the past (the cause), and as a result, they now struggle with trust (the effect).

Reflect on a past event that significantly shaped your emotional landscape. How have its effects manifested in your life choices?

Adding Consequences to the Mix

Now let's add another factor into the cause-and-effect relationship: consequences.

CAUSE + EFFECT + CONSEQUENCES = EMOTIONAL BAGGAGE

To break this down:

The cause is the event or experience that triggers an emotional reaction. The effect is the emotion we feel in response to that event.

The consequences are the actions we take as a result of those emotions – these actions are what ultimately shape our emotional baggage.

The consequences belong to us – not to the person or event that may have caused the initial pain. And if these actions and emotions remain unresolved and continue repeating, they contribute to our emotional baggage.

For Example:

Cause: Growing up in a household where I was neglected (cause).

Effect: As a result, I felt insecure and unworthy (effect).

Consequences: Because of these feelings, I may have avoided relationships or sabotaged opportunities, believing I wasn't good enough (consequence).

When we repeat these patterns without addressing the root cause, we create emotional baggage that repeats itself and weighs us down.

> **What consequences of your emotional reactions are you currently facing? How can you approach them with a view of healing?**

Adding Consequences to the Mix

Now I am going to add another factor into the cause-and-effect relationship, and that is consequences.

CAUSE + EFFECT + CONSEQUENCES = EMOTIONAL BAGGAGE

What consequences of your emotional reactions are you currently facing? How can you approach these with a view toward healing?

If we know that the cause is the experience or event and the effects are the emotions, then the actions we take because of those emotions are the consequences. These consequences belong to us and not the individual or event that may be the root cause. This formula, if unresolved and repeated consistently, is emotional baggage.

Imagine what a child goes through when a parent consistently tells them they are worthless, stupid, and will never amount to anything. What is the effect? In the case of my middle brother and sister, they felt worthless, stupid, and as if they would never amount to anything. That is the effect. The addition of their consequences solidified their emotional damage. They just wanted to be loved, accepted, and to belong. They, in turn, met friends who felt the same way. What is the one thing kids do when they are desperate to belong? They seem to gravitate toward consequences that will seemingly protect them from the cause-and-effect relationship. They want their family to reach out and love them. They want to be heard. By the age of 13, my brother was in serious legal trouble as well as addicted to serious drugs and alcohol. My sister, by the age of 14, was cutting school, smoking pot as well as experimenting with other drugs, and hanging with the toughest, scariest groups of girls I remember from school. These actions were her consequences – not a reflection of our parents' choices, but hers alone. The more the root cause of verbal and physical abuse occurred, the deeper the emotions, the greater the attachment to the consequences, and the more embedded the emotional baggage. To cope or compensate, both my brother and sister said that drugs relieved them, if only for a small amount of time, of the effect or emotions. That is where they felt safe and had no pain. Drugs gave them a sense of control—control that they didn't have at home. That's where they felt safe and free from pain. Drugs gave them a temporary sense of control – a control they lacked at home. But like the escape they provided, that control was an illusion. In reality, they had no control at all. In fact, now they were being controlled by two things: a destructive home environment and drugs, which in the end, resulted in even less control from where they started

> Consider how your own past experiences have influenced your emotional responses. Are there specific events that still trigger strong emotions today?

With this understanding, it is safe to say that without reconciliation, negative emotions are triggered and grow stronger roots as time goes by. However, the stronger the root, the harder it is to release the emotion tied to it, thus the consequences get greater and more dire as one grows older. Life doesn't seem fair at this point because you are suffering the consequences you created but may not have caused. It seems backward, but the root cause is no longer the problem; the root emotions you carry are, and the only way to move past it is to reconcile with the root cause. So how do we do that? Remember, root causes are the events and experiences of the past.

Exploring Common Root Causes

In my family alone, we have experienced many: abandonment, child molestation, physical abuse, verbal abuse, neglect, traumatic events, divorce, bullying, peer pressure, and relationship conflicts that go beyond divorce. If I were to illustrate how each of these causes manifested in my family, it would be an extremely long book, and that is not the purpose. The point is, causes like these are all too common in family culture today, and the consequences can be life and death. Add the internet as a vehicle for this formula to manifest, and it becomes a recipe for disaster. If our children continue to be exposed to these types of causes, then what will our society look like? What will our children's adult lives look like? Since more often than not, emotional baggage begins its journey in childhood, let's take a hard look at ourselves as adults and ask: What can we do better? How can we be better? How can I break the cycle? If not for ourselves, then for the sake of our children. Wouldn't that be a great motivator?

The Danger of Generational Baggage

In my experience, the most challenging aspect of emotional baggage is that its root cause can be limitless. No parent sets out to burden their child with emotional baggage. Yet, without realizing it, some parents make the mistake of having children with the unconscious hope that this new life will provide a fresh start or save a troubled relationship. They believe that the innocence and unconditional love of a child will somehow fix everything—that everyone will be happy, and that a child will bring joy where there has been pain.

But this places an impossible burden on the child, one they never asked for. It's like a teacher telling students on the first day of school, "You're starting this semester with an F, and it's up to you to work your way up to an A," rather than, "You're starting with an A, and it's up to you to maintain it." A child can bring joy into a family's life, yes, but that joy should be an extension of the love and happiness two people already share—not the solution to their emotional struggles.

This is what I call generational baggage. When we expect a child to heal what's broken between two adults, it places an undue burden on them. The child does not become the fix, but often ends up feeling broken themselves.

> Think about the generational patterns in your family. How have these patterns influenced your behavior and beliefs?

Personal Anecdotes: Generational Baggage in My Family

There is an old wives' tale that states, if you are a girl, how a man treats his mother is how he will treat you, or the relationship between a father and a daughter will determine the relationship a woman will look for in a man. Yes, this seems very old school, but there is truth to it. At least it was certainly true in my family. I have already mentioned what type of man my father was. To put it lightly, he was very disrespectful to my mom. In turn, my brothers, as teenagers, were disrespectful to my mom and carried that into their own personal relationships and marriages. As for my sister and me, we watched and learned how to be treated by a man from our mother, which meant we strived for approval from a man, not love. I myself married a man who represented my father. So much so, my first husband, like my father, was an only child, had no respect for his mom, and was a bully. As if that wasn't enough, my first husband's birthday was the same day as my father's. How crazy is that? You would think that with all I have been through regarding my family, I wouldn't fall into that trap, but without reconciliation, it took me three marriages to realize that, although what seemed on face value to be three very different personalities, my husbands all had one thing in common: they had a controlling nature, and I was always trying to prove myself worthy. I don't blame them. Who they were was a result of their experiences. Who I am was a result of my experiences.

> Reflect on your own relationships. How might past family dynamics be influencing your current interactions with others?

Currently, I'm married to a man who is the complete opposite of controlling. Now, I find myself in control, and if I'm honest, it's uncomfortable. It's not about him—it's about me. This kind of marriage, this kind of love, feels unfamiliar. Unconditional love? I didn't even know what that looked like. And sometimes I wonder, am I even capable of loving unconditionally?

When you've spent so long in unhealthy environments, stepping into what should be a healthy one can feel deeply unsettling. It's like being on unfamiliar ground. And the question that keeps circling in my mind is: Has the pendulum swung too far in the other direction? The goal in any marriage isn't about extremes—it's about balance, finding a space between two people where both can thrive without the pendulum swinging too far in either direction.

The truth is, I haven't found that balance yet. I still struggle. But the difference now is that I see the pendulum. I recognize when it's off course, and I'm learning to make adjustments. I'm not where I need to be, but I'm not where I was either.

Generational Baggage Beyond Parents

Generational baggage is not limited to parents. It can go back generations before our parents. After all, our parents are the way they are because of their upbringing. Culture and society also play a role in generational baggage. Behaviors that may have been considered acceptable or tolerable back then are not accepted now. For example, my father was a womanizer and cheated on my mom several times, and his father was the same way. My grandmother didn't like it, but she felt that in spite of my grandfather's behavior, she was the one he loved, and that was enough.

My father, on the other hand, had affairs not because he loved my mother, but because he didn't. Divorce was still taboo back in the '50s and '60s. No one dared divorce over an affair because, up until the mid-20th century, adultery was considered a crime, and New York was one of the 16 states that had that law. Even though it was rare for a person to be tried for adultery, I can only imagine the fear that men would have if their jilted wife were to find out. While my father reluctantly stayed married to my mom, my mother fought to be loved by him. It wasn't until the 1970s, twenty-three years into their marriage, when society said it was okay to divorce, that my parents finally divorced. Sadly, six lives were emotionally damaged and lost in the process.

Impact of Societal Changes on Generational Baggage

Before the 1970s, the divorce rate hovered around 35%. But in 1972, California passed a new law allowing divorce based on irreconcilable differences—a concept that quickly spread to other states. By 1979, the divorce rate had skyrocketed to 53%. Can you imagine how many couples must have been waiting for a way out of their marriages?

To put it into perspective, the children born during that time were part of the Baby Boomer generation, of which my siblings and I are members. I'm no historian, but looking at these statistics, it seems clear that Baby Boomers were the first true "generation of divorce." Much like Gen Z is known for being the technology generation because they were born into an era of rapid tech growth, Baby Boomers were born into an era when dealing with emotional issues often meant fleeing, not fighting to resolve them.

For years, the divorce rate remained high, fluctuating between 47% and 53% until the turn of the century. While it's encouraging that divorce rates have decreased significantly since the late 1990s, it's worth noting that the desire to marry has also waned. Many people now avoid marriage altogether, which raises questions about how we've learned—or failed to learn—from the past.

As a child watching my parents endure 23 years of a tortured marriage, I swore that if I ever found myself unhappy in a relationship, I wouldn't wait that long. And I didn't. Until my current marriage, none of my previous marriages lasted more than two and a half years.

For a long time, I carried shame over the fact that I've been married four times and divorced three. But when I open up to friends and other women about this, I'm often met with laughter and confessions like, "Oh, me too! I've been divorced twice or three times!" It's made me wonder—are we really evolving into a healthier society, or are we just carrying our baggage forward, making poor choices when it comes to lifelong partners?

The children of our baby boomer generation, on the other hand—the generation of millennials—changed that. Because of our flight instead of fight conundrum, I believe too many millennial children were raised in single parent homes, resulting in millennials either marrying later in life or not at all. The definition of family would never be the same. For millennials and Generation X, the divorce rate decreased. Of course! These generations are not quick to get married like previous generations. These generations either have live in life partners or get married late. In addition, this generation is having fewer and fewer children or having children much later in their lives. From generation to generation of emotional baggage, it does not surprise me that now, more than ever, we need to get a grip on who we are, what we want, and how we can not only make our lives better but also positively impact the lives of those around us.

Reconciling with the Past

So let's go back to where it began. Root causes are events or experiences that occur in our past, which trigger root emotions that, if left unreconciled, equate to emotional baggage. Once again, we see that key word unreconciled. To reconcile something, you have got to give it closure, and there are many ways to do that. In my experience, there is no smoking gun resolution here. For me, I did many things to overcome my baggage. I focused on my faith, went to therapy, educated myself in leadership and self-help books, surrounded myself with positive influences, and allowed myself to be uncomfortable while growing from the inside out. Everyone is different, so everyone's healing journey will be different. Knowing to ask for help is the first step. Not necessarily help from your friends. Friends can sometimes be enablers because they don't know how to help. You want to seek the help of a professional or a person(s) whom you want to aspire to be like one day. Ask questions. Learn a little, then do a little. One step at a time. One day at a time.

Faith as a Source of Strength

The most important lesson I learned about root causes is that when you seek closure, know that it doesn't necessarily require two people—you and the person who caused the emotional damage. It just requires you and the ability to have compassion and forgiveness. The best way I knew how to do this was when I truly understood the Lord's Prayer. When Jesus taught his disciples how to pray, it was in a group setting, so the prayer is written in plural:

Our Father who art in heaven, hallowed be thy name. The kingdom come; thy will be done on earth as it is in heaven. Give us this day our daily bread; and forgive for our sins, as we forgive those who have sinned against us. And lead us not into temptation but deliver us from evil.
Amen

This prayer is very powerful on its own, but when I find myself alone with God, feeling that I don't know what to pray, I change "us" to "I." Using the I, for me makes it personal, just me and God and provides me even more strength to accept, forgive, and let go. Here is how I switch things up:

"My Father who lives in heaven, how great is your name. Let your kingdom come, let your will be done in my life on earth as it is in heaven. Give me this day my daily bread, and forgive me my sins, as I will forgive those who have sinned against me. And, Father, lead me not into temptation, but deliver me from the emotions/temptations that bind me, and deliver me from evil and the pain of my past." In Your Name, Amen.

Honestly, praying the Lord's Prayer like this gives me the strength to not only forgive but also sets the stage for how I am to move forward. The Lord's Prayer becomes personal and speaks to God when I can't find the words myself. I can't imagine closure without faith. I am sure some may disagree, but as for me, my closure did not come from my parents admitting they were wrong and apologizing. Closure for me came from within – which is where all closure should begin. When my father died, it was his wish that I be the only child "allowed" at his funeral. (Even in my father's death, he wanted his kids to hate each other.) My father left me to honor this wish, and I was extremely conflicted. Do I choose his wishes over telling my siblings? Do I honor him, or do I honor my siblings? Given the complicated situation my siblings would have walked into, I felt it best to honor my dad's wishes. To this day, I am still conflicted by my decision. However, just after he was buried, I called one of my brothers. At first, he was very accepting of the situation, but as the reality of my father's death set in, one by one my siblings really hated me for it. I was disowned once again. They felt they hadn't received the closure they believed they rightly deserved – or at the very least, they wanted to have the last word. Imagine living for sixty years, waiting for the root cause – the person where all the emotional baggage began – to say, "I'm sorry please forgive me." The hard truth is, closure is not always a two way street. Therefore, it is so important to establish closure from within your heart first. That is where forgiveness lives. Any closure you get outside of that is a bonus.

> **Consider how your faith or personal beliefs can support your journey toward emotional healing.**

What if the person you need closure from is no longer in your life? What then? Don't spend your life waiting, hoping, and thinking you will get it from the person(s) who wronged you. It is a slow drip of wasteful heartache that you are allowing to cultivate in your heart. Remember, closure of the root cause must first come from within you, and only you can do that. Can I get a BIG AMEN to that?!

As we conclude this chapter, it's important to acknowledge the profound impact that our unresolved emotional baggage has on our lives. The journey of identifying these deep-rooted issues is not just about understanding our past but about taking the first steps toward healing. By recognizing the causes, effects, and consequences of our emotional baggage, we gain the insight needed to begin the process of reconciliation. This journey may be challenging, but it is essential for breaking the cycle of pain and dysfunction that has affected not only us but also those around us.

Through reflection, self-awareness, and a commitment to growth, we can start to dismantle the emotional barriers that have held us back. Remember, the power to change lies within us, and the process of healing begins with a willingness to confront our past and embrace the path to emotional freedom.

In the next chapter, we will delve deeper into the broader impact of emotional baggage on various aspects of our lives. Chapter 4, "The Impact of Emotional Baggage," will explore how unresolved issues ripple through our personal decisions, relationships, and even our physical and mental health. We will examine how the baggage we carry influences our choices in the workplace, our interactions with others, and our overall well-being. As we continue this journey, the focus will shift from identifying our emotional baggage to understanding its far-reaching consequences and learning how to mitigate its effects on our lives.

Chapter 4

The Impact of Emotional Baggage

"Come to me, all you who are weary and burdened, and I will give you rest."
— *Matthew 11:28 (NIV)*

Emotional baggage has undoubtedly impacted my life in numerous ways. Previously, I have discussed how emotional baggage has manifested in my life through guilt, regret, grief, lack of trust, low self-esteem, unresolved anger, and fear of abandonment. These factors have significantly influenced my decision making from adolescence into adulthood. The truth is, we all carry emotional baggage. If we are living, we have dealt with some level of emotional baggage and held on to its effects. What makes us unique is the range in which emotional baggage settles into who we are, ranging from mild dysfunction to severe mental illness and even, in some cases, death.

As I reflect on the many paths I've walked, I realize that each step was often weighted by the unseen but deeply felt burdens of my past. Decisions that seemed rational at the time were, in fact, influenced by unresolved issues I had yet to confront. The complexity of this baggage is that it doesn't just affect us in isolated moments—it accumulates, impacting every facet of our lives, often in ways we don't immediately recognize.

> Reflect on how emotional baggage has influenced your major life decisions. How has it shaped your path and your relationships?

The Ripple Effect of Emotional Baggage

Two major decisions in my life were heavily influenced by my emotional baggage, both from home and the military. The first was getting married during my first tour of duty in the military, which unfortunately led to me cutting my service short. I had committed to a four-year term but only managed to finish three. Let me just say, that was never the plan. I loved the military and everything that I was achieving. At the time, joining the Army felt like the best decision I'd ever made. I had ambitions of making it my career, aiming for a twenty-year tenure. But instead, I found myself succumbing to my emotional baggage.

My first husband, a German national and my person trainer, embodied many of the qualities I admired in my father, which drew me to him. After a year of dating him, we got married and not long after, I became pregnant. However, much like my parents' relationship ours quickly deteriorated – this time even before my daughter was born. Life was repeating itself. But unlike my parents who waited 23 years, I left much sooner. At just 3 months pregnant, I moved back into the barracks.

It wasn't until after we were married that I discovered the depth of his steroid use (his drug of choice), not to mention the legal troubles he brought into our marriage. The decision to marry this man ultimately affected not only my military career but also my sense of stability, leaving me isolated in a foreign country.

The decision to be with Klaus was driven by a deep-seated need for security, a sense of belonging I felt I lacked growing up. The admiration I had for my father, despite his flaws, led me to seek out partners who mirrored his qualities—strength, confidence, and a commanding presence. However, I failed to recognize the underlying issues that came sometimes can accompany these traits, such as control and emotional unavailability, which would later unravel the stability I so desperately sought.

I vividly remember the first time I met him. The gym's fluorescent lights buzzed overhead as I watched him lift weights with effortless precision. His chiseled features and confident demeanor captivated me, reminding me of the security and strength I had always sought in my father. Within months, we were living together, and a year later, we were married. Deep down, I knew living together wasn't the best choice for me. But instead of following my instincts, I gave into my emotional baggage and pushed for marriage, believing it would somehow right a wrong.

The early days were filled with joy and anticipation, but the honeymoon phase didn't last. His hidden life began to surface, and discovering his excessive steroid use and legal troubles hit me like a punch to the gut, shattering my hopes for a stable military career and family life.

> Consider how the need for security or validation has influenced your past decisions. How might your emotional baggage have shaped these choices?

The second major decision I made was driven by my desire to give my daughter a better life than I had. Despite the tumultuous relationship with her father, I reconciled with him, believing it was the right thing to do for her. However, just three months before Brittney was born, Klaus made it clear he wanted nothing to do with her—ever. For him, simply knowing the gender and that she was healthy was enough.

Originally, my plan was to stay in the military as a single parent and move forward with my next tour of duty, which would be stateside. But once again, I caved. I convinced myself that for the sake of my daughter, I should abandon that plan—leave the military—and try to fix my marriage.

That decision only led to further instability and, eventually, another separation. This time, though, the consequences were even greater. Looking back, I can see how my emotional baggage didn't just affect my life—it also impacted my daughter's. It's a stark reminder of how unresolved issues can ripple through generations.

In trying to provide my daughter with the stability I lacked, I overlooked the importance of my own well-being. I believed that by keeping her father in her life, I was giving her what I never had—a complete family. But in doing so, I subjected both of us to continued emotional turmoil. It took years for me to understand that stability doesn't come from external circumstances alone; it must be cultivated within, free from the unresolved baggage of the past.

Emotional Baggage in the Workplace

We often hear advice to leave personal problems at the door when entering the workplace. However, the challenge lies not in leaving the problems behind, but in managing the emotions associated with them. Emotions are intrinsic to our DNA and influence how we perceive and interact with others in the workplace. According to Louise Altman, "Once in the workplace, many of us tend to view workplace relationships primarily through the prism of our past experiences." For instance, a boss may remind us of a critical parent, or a coworker might evoke sibling rivalry. These associations can lead to significant stress and dissatisfaction.

Throughout my career, I've left several jobs because the environment triggered the unresolved emotional baggage. For example, I once quit what I still consider my favorite job because I was no longer the "teacher's pet" and couldn't handle the pressure of establishing my success on my own. I was dependent on recognition – something I didn't receive as a child and desperately craved as an adult. I didn't truly need it, but my emotional baggage did. This pattern repeated itself in almost every job I had. I was constantly seeking external validation instead of addressing my internal and emotional needs. Recognizing these patterns is crucial for breaking the cycle and finding satisfaction in professional settings

Reflect on a time when your emotional baggage influenced your interactions at work. How did it affect your
performance and relationships with colleagues?

The workplace is not just a place of employment; it's a micro-
cosm where our unresolved issues often resurface. I've encountered
bosses whose authoritarian styles mirrored the controlling nature
of my father, triggering feelings of inadequacy and anxiety. These
emotional responses would often lead to a decline in my performance and eventual resignation, perpetuating a cycle of instability
in my professional life. It wasn't until I began addressing these deep
seated issues that I could see the patterns clearly and start to make
changes.

Impact on Relationships

Unhealthy relationships from childhood often spill into adulthood, affecting social interactions, work dynamics, and marriages.
Emotional baggage is a major factor in dysfunctional relationships.
In my immediate family of six (two parents and four children),
we collectively experienced thirteen, nine ended in divorce and
one by the involuntary passing of my sister's second husband. This
statistic highlights the profound effect of emotional baggage on
relationships. The cycle of dysfunction continued as we repeatedly
sought partners who reflected the unresolved issues from our past.

Two specific triggers I identified in my relationships were
codependency and controlling behavior. My mother was code-
pendent, always trying to appease or fix my father. This pattern
influenced my own relationships, as I married controlling men,

seeking the security and validation I lacked as a child. Over time, I too became controlling, limiting my heart to protect myself from further pain.

I remember how my mother would go to great lengths to keep my father happy, even at her own expense. This behavior seemed normal to me, and I carried it into my relationships. I sought out men who I thought needed "fixing", believing I could earn their love through sacrifice. But the idea of "fixing" was an illusion. It stemmed from the emotional detachment I grew up with, pushing me to try to "fix" them. Much like my relationship with my father, I was determined to move heaven and earth to prove I was worth their love and commitment. The more I reached for emotion and commitment, the worse my relationships became. I had become my mother – the very woman I once resented for doing the same thing. It took years of self-reflection and therapy to understand this destructive pattern.

> **How have your past relationships affected your current ones? Reflect on the patterns you see and how they relate to your emotional baggage.**

Relationships aren't limited to marriages – they include friendships as well. Some people compensate for unhealthy home environments by forming numerous friendships outside the home. Misery loves company, so the friends you keep matter. While some friends perpetuate the dysfunctional cycle, others can inspire you to grow beyond it. Seek out the latter. Be mindful of those, especially children, who have no friends at all. For parents reading this, a lack of friends is a significant warning sign. That's when kids need your love and trust the most. Additionally, some people bond over shared emotional baggage, much like my siblings did, which can continue the cycle of dysfunction. It is essential to seek friendships with those who encourage growth and positive change.

Throughout life, we often find ourselves drawn to two types of people: those who are catabolic, seeing the glass half empty, and those who are anabolic, viewing it as half full. Catabolic friendships keep unresolved emotional baggage alive, while anabolic friends challenge us to rise above it. I often felt like I was caught between Dr. Jekyll and Mr. Hyde, constantly torn between good and evil. I learned to navigate both sides, but this back-and-forth kept me from moving forward.

When I gravitated toward catabolic people, my emotional baggage cemented itself even further, growing stronger and gaining more power. When I could no longer handle it, I would seek out anabolic people – often older and wiser – to help me get unstuck and move forward. But the cycle would repeat and the catabolic energy within me always seemed to win. These relationships, while comforting in their familiarity, ultimately kept me trapped in patterns of dysfunction.

> **Consider your friendships and relationships. Are they helping you grow or are they reinforcing old patterns?**

Sexual trauma can also significantly impact emotional baggage. This type of trauma devalues a person and is challenging to overcome without professional help. The severity of such trauma goes beyond mild dysfunction and requires addressing by a specialist to prevent long term detrimental effects. I've seen trauma buried so deeply that a person may block the memory, but the "baggage" continues to resurface, leaving them confused about why it keeps happening. This is why seeking professional help is crucial. Recognizing a pattern of self-destruction without understanding its cause is debilitating. True healing, recovery, and change can only begin once the root cause is uncovered.

Emotional baggage can manifest physically, causing health issues such as headaches, back pain, or stomach problems. Prolonged stress from unresolved emotional baggage can lead to more severe conditions like high blood pressure, heart disease, stroke, obesity, diabetes, and eating disorders. It is not surprising, considering that holding onto emotional pain can have a profound impact on our physical well-being. For example, I have struggled with IBS-D while another family member has experienced eating disorders and severe digestive issues related to anxiety.,

I remember the countless nights spent curled up in bed, my stomach in knots, unable to eat or sleep. The physical pain was a constant reminder of the emotional turmoil I was trying to suppress. It wasn't until I began addressing my emotional baggage that my IBS symptoms started to improve.

> **Think about the physical manifestations of emotional baggage in your life. How has stress or unresolved pain affected your health?**

Mental health is also significantly affected by emotional baggage. Low self-esteem, trauma, physical and mental abuse, and even suicidal thoughts or attempts can result from unresolved issues. My family's experience with mental health challenges, particularly my mother's psychotic episodes and a suicide attempt, illustrates the severe impact of emotional baggage on mental health. These episodes were terrifying and highlighted the urgent need for addressing emotional pain.

My mother's psychotic episodes were some of the most harrowing experiences of my life. The terror and confusion I felt during those moments left deep emotional scars that took years to heal. These events served as stark reminders of how unresolved emotional pain can lead to severe mental health crises.

One of the most traumatic events involved a suicide attempt - or at least, that is how it seemed. Thankfully, I wasn't there to witness it, but when I got home, I was met with two conflicting versions of the story which remain a mystery to this day. In one version, my mother faked the attempt during another psychotic episode, driving her car at a slow speed into the telephone pole at the end of our driveway and claiming to have swallowed a large number of pills: all to get my father's attention. In the other version, she truly intended to end her life. To this day, which version is true depends on who you ask. Either way, the outcome was devasting.

The incident felt like Mt. Everest of all the destruction that accumulated in our home. The damage was irreparable, and we were each left to figure out how to cope with it on our own. My relationship with my mother was never the same, and the resentment I felt toward my family seemed unbreakable.

As we close this chapter, it's crucial to understand that the impact of emotional baggage extends far beyond our internal world. It influences our relationships, our careers, our health, and ultimately our entire life trajectory. The process of recognizing and addressing this baggage is not just about healing past wounds—it's about reclaiming the power to shape our future. By acknowledging how these unresolved emotions have shaped our lives, we open the door to transformation and growth. Remember, the journey toward emotional freedom is ongoing, but each step taken with intention brings us closer to a life unburdened by the past.

In the next chapter, we will explore the transformation process in greater depth. Chapter 5, titled "Breaking Free! The Transformation Process," will guide you through the steps necessary to move from acknowledgment to action. This chapter will delve into the importance of recognizing triggers, the power of forgiveness, and how to live a life filled with intention and purpose. As you embark on this next stage of your journey, prepare to embrace the freedom that comes from letting go of the past and stepping into a future defined by your resilience and strength.

Chapter 5

Breaking Free! – The Transformation Process

"He heals the brokenhearted and binds up their wounds."
— Psalm 143:3 (NIV)

The journey to break free from emotional baggage is a transformation process. It begins with the recognition of the burden we carry, followed by the courage to confront and overcome it. Emotional baggage influences our decisions, relationships, and overall well-being. This chapter explores the steps involved in transitioning from carrying emotional burdens to living a life of freedom and growth. By embracing this process, we open ourselves to healing and transformation. The journey may be challenging, but the rewards are immense, leading to a life filled with peace, purpose, and joy.

The Power of Acknowledgment

I have heard it said that the only way to solve a problem is to first recognize that you have one. When it comes to emotional baggage, this statement carries significant weight. Acknowledgment is the beginning of hope, and hope is the foundation of all possibilities. With hope, we start to acknowledge our burdens and begin the journey of transformation. How many times do we need to acknowledge our baggage before taking steps to free ourselves from it? Hopefully, less is more. As for me, I asked myself this question too many times. The good news is that you are asking that question, which means something inside you wants to be healed. Listen to that voice because your best self is trying to break free.

Transitioning from emotional baggage to a healthy mindset involves acknowledging and processing your emotions, practicing self-care, and developing resilience. Allow yourself to feel your emotions. The more you keep them inside, the more you deny your true self the chance to live. During this process, avoid judging your emotions as good or bad. Being too hard on yourself is wasted energy and keeps your emotional baggage alive. Wouldn't it be great if we had a loud alarm that warned us when we were letting our baggage get the best of us? Life would be much simpler, right? While we don't have a physical alarm, we do have triggers. Identifying these triggers helps us recognize when we are entering our world of emotional baggage. With training and intentional living, these alarms start off subtly but become more obvious as we understand ourselves better, giving us the opportunity to change course. It's important to remember that acknowledging our baggage is not a one-time event but a continuous process of self-awareness and growth.

Recognizing Triggers

I remember the first time I learned about these so-called "alarms" or "triggers." It was when I decided to see a therapist after my second failed marriage. My therapist and I discussed how my choice of men often reminded me of my father. She advised, "If you find yourself saying, 'Wow, this guy reminds me of my dad,' run to the hills and take a different path!" Listen to what your conscience is telling you; it's often right. This thought process worked for a while, but because I wasn't consistent in my "discovery journey," I eventually made the same mistake. The next man I chose to spend my life with had many layers, and the "father" layer didn't show up at first. By the time I recognized it, I was already very emotionally invested in the relationship.

Another mistake I made during my transition process was deciding to move in with my boyfriends. What complicated this issue was that I was a single mom. Looking back, these were not good decisions for me or my daughter. If I had a boyfriend, 8 out of 10 times, I would move in. Even though I wanted more for myself, I always sold myself short and moved in. I gave up my self-preservation and my identity. I always thought of these relationships as a fresh start and subconsciously ignored the signs. This was the baggage that my daughter really resented and caused a lot of turmoil between us. In my mind, I was trying to give her the white picket fence life I didn't have. I also had every intention of marrying the person I moved in with, which justified my decision to myself. What my daughter saw was different. She saw a woman who didn't believe in herself, didn't want to be strong on her own, and felt she needed a man to be happy or complete. All my daughter wanted was me, but I was too busy trying to fill a void that she didn't create. She wanted me to step up and be the woman she knew I could be. Her entire childhood was built on this scenario. Remember when I mentioned that baggage travels from generation to generation? Well, there it was. Brittney was 16 years old, and she saw me as weak and unreliable, exactly how I saw my mom.

I will never forget the day she finally let it all out and let me have it. I was now married for the third time, and the marriage had turned ugly. She was disgusted with me and incredibly angry. As we were driving up the driveway, she let it all out. I had no idea her frustration with me was based on years of disappointment in my decisions regarding men. She felt I was putting my relationships with men before my relationship with her by moving in with them before developing myself. She felt like the third wheel in my life. Hearing this from her was gut-wrenching. Everything I thought I was doing right and for her turned out to be incredibly wrong. Don't get me wrong; I did the responsible things well. I provided for her, surrounded her with good, well-rounded people who became good friends to both of us, and gave her life tools that set her up for success. However, I missed the most important thing a child could ever want—the emotion of love. Since I never experienced love as a child, I didn't know how to show love as a parent. Of course, I loved her, but the responsibility of being a parent trumped the expression of love. I showed her my love by being responsible for her, not by being loving. Again, there it was: generational baggage passed on to me that I was now passing on to my daughter. This was truly my defining moment and the true beginning of my long-term transition process.

During this time, I learned that I was so focused on trying to live a white picket fence life, but I wasn't a white picket fence person. In my mind, a white picket fence meant a mother, a father, kids, and a decent home, all happy together within that picket fence. What Brittney taught me was that we, even if it was just her and I, were family, and that in itself was a white picket fence. It didn't matter how big the home was or whether there was a husband or father in the picture. What mattered was that at our very core, we were our picket fence. This realization was profound and shifted my perspective on what it means to create a loving and supportive home environment.

Imagine learning the most important lesson in your life from your teenage child. I guess there is justification for the phrase "out of the mouths of babes." My experience with my daughter inspired my first book idea, "Raising Brittney Raising Mom," which I have yet to write. Since my daughter is now in the movie business, I think she would rather direct the movie instead of helping me write the book. It is so important as parents to listen to our kids through their actions and words. They tell us so much about what they need but don't have the maturity to understand exactly what that is. That is our job as parents. If children are rebelling, even in the smallest way, it may be a sign that we, as parents, need to reevaluate ourselves and put our kids before our baggage. I don't know of a greater incentive for me to genuinely begin the transition from being trapped in my baggage to letting go than my daughter. I only wish I had recognized it a lot sooner. Thankfully, God is good, and today Brittney and I are solid as a rock!

The Role of Forgiveness and Letting Go.

When I was on my transition journey, forgiveness and letting go had to come first because this is where emotional baggage sustains itself. Forgiveness, or one's inability to forgive, is based on feelings: feelings of fear, being hurt, emotional pain, rejection, or not being good enough. All these things are related to fear, and fear is a feeling. Once we recognize that feelings come and go and don't represent us at our core, we begin to empower ourselves toward healing. In Tal Ben-Shahar's book, "Choose the Life You Want," he writes, "To forgive in Sanskrit is to untie an emotional knot. When we forgive, we untie an emotional knot and unclog the emotional system. We release the free flow of emotions and are able to feel the anger, disappointment, fear, as well as the pain, compassion, and joy. Holding a grudge is like continuously pulling on the knot, making it tighter. Letting go of the grudge is like loosening our grip, making the knot easier to untie." For me, replacing the word "grudge" with "baggage" makes Ben-Shahar's statement even more valuable.

Author David Ridge says, "True forgiveness is not an action after the fact; it is an attitude with which you enter each moment." At twenty-five years of age, I could never have approached my father without forgiving him BEFORE I went to see him. The thing often misunderstood about forgiveness is it is often confused with closure for both parties involved. The fact of the matter is forgiveness is about you moving forward with or without the person on the other side of that baggage. If we wait to see the other person to discuss the hurt and pain involved and to let them know "we forgive them," we could be waiting a long time. Many times, the person on the other side of that damage doesn't care whether you forgive them or not. If they are a narcissist, they will more than likely not even acknowledge they did something wrong or hurt you. Then what do you do? Dig in your heels until you finally break them? That is not going to happen. In the case of my father, he didn't care if any of his kids forgave him. Honestly, he never felt he needed to be forgiven. It just wasn't important to him. We weren't important to him. So where does that leave a child? Sadly, in a lot of pain that will stay with them for their entire life unless they say to themselves, "Regardless of how you feel about me, I still forgive you." Often, this is not a face-to-face conversation. This is a conversation you have with yourself or with God.

Believe me, I have tried to let go and forgive without God, but what I have found is that letting go without spiritual forgiveness is just not sustainable. When I did try to just forgive for forgiveness's sake, I found I was burying my thoughts and feelings so deep that it gave the appearance of letting go, but in reality, burying pain is not releasing pain. In fact, it is the exact opposite. Burying pain becomes more volatile when it rears its ugly head again, and I was far worse off the second or third time around. When I was able to forgive my father, only then could I be in a conversation with him. At that point, nothing he could say would hurt me, but instead, inform me as to why he was the way he was. If you get that far, you may find yourself replacing pain with healing.

Forgiveness with the help of God also allowed me to forgive without expectations. I never expected my dad to say he was sorry or to change the way he was. I accepted him for who he was in the present and never held him accountable for the past. If I had continued to live in that past, healing would never have taken place for me. Forgiveness was about me moving forward. What my dad did was on him, and I truly believe that was his cross to bear. There was no need to put his baggage on mine anymore. That is what forgiveness does. It gets rid of you carrying someone else's baggage. Imagine being empowered like that. I was able to accept him for who he was while not allowing him to treat me as he did. I had a new attitude, and he sensed it. Only then could he tell me his side of the story, his pain, his regrets, and his truth. It was the beginning of healing. I was free to choose how I would handle any relationship with my father. He no longer had that unhealthy hold on me.

Had I never had the opportunity to reconcile with my dad, I still would have forgiven him because it was for my sake. Not forgiving him meant that what he had done to our family still had a hold on me, and I wouldn't have been able to move forward. I must say this would have been harder but necessary. Forgiveness without reconciliation makes closure and letting go harder but not impossible. That is why my ability to forgive is based on my faith and not on my human intellect. One thing my faith in God has taught me is that as much as we want forgiveness from others, we must also forgive others and ourselves.

Forgiveness is so powerful; so much so that you can find many quotes about forgiveness. These quotes are transformative for me. I hope they are for you as well:

- *"All major religious traditions carry basically the same message: that is love, compassion, and forgiveness. The important thing is they should be part of our daily lives."* — *Dalai Lama*

- *"Forgiveness is not an occasional act; it is a permanent attitude."* — *Martin Luther King Jr.*

- *"To be a Christian means to forgive the inexcusable because God has forgiven the inexcusable in you."* — *C.S. Lewis*

- *"Forgiveness liberates the soul. It removes fear. That is why it is such a powerful weapon."* — *Nelson Mandela*

- *"Forgive others not because they deserve forgiveness but because you deserve peace."* — *Jonathan Huie*

- *"I forgive myself and set myself free."* — Louise Hay
- *"Forgiveness is not always easy. At times, it feels more painful than the wound we suffered to forgive the one that inflicted it. And yet, there is no peace without forgiveness."* — Marianne Williamson

Putting Your Thoughts into Actions

Letting go and forgiveness are easier said than done. However, this is what makes the transition from emotional baggage to emotional freedom so powerful and worth the journey. John Maxwell says, "To know yourself is to grow yourself." We all desire to matter, to be significant, to be heard, and to be loved, but first, you have to love yourself. Holding onto emotional baggage hinders the very thing you desire. Have you thought about what your life would look like if you made the transition from baggage to freedom? Write it down. What is holding you back? Write it down. Who is holding you back and why? What are you afraid of? Why? Write it down!

Paint your picture. Imagine big! What is the dream? If you were free from your emotional baggage, what would you do with your life? What would your career look like? Your marriage and family? Would you have different friends or make new friends? Create your vision board. Take some time to breathe it in and own it. Turn your vision into goals and then figure out the pros and cons of each goal. You may find that your biggest obstacle is you. Confronting your baggage is not fun, but it is rewarding. Confronting our baggage means getting comfortable with being uncomfortable. First, do the thing we all avoid when it comes to dealing with emotional baggage—get emotional! Cry it out. Talk it out. This means being vulnerable, which is the hardest thing above all, even above forgiveness. To forgive or be forgiven, you must allow yourself to be vulnerable. Tear down that wall!

In his book, "Choose the Life You Want: The Mindful Way to Happiness," Tal Ben-Shahar quotes author Brené Brown: "Vulnerability is the core of shame, fear, and our struggle for worthiness, but it is also the birthplace of joy, creativity, belonging, and love." Ben-Shahar mentions a study by Brown on people with high self-esteem. In this study, Brown states, "Vulnerability comes at a price—it can hurt a lot! But the cost is negligible compared to the cost we pay when we suppress part of our humanity. When we don't allow ourselves to be vulnerable, we also suppress our joy and happiness and the potential to cultivate deep and meaningful connections in our life." I couldn't have said it better myself.

Confronting your emotional baggage is essential in the transformation process, and it must be intentional. At some point, you may say, "I will try and let go," but trying is not enough. If you commit to being uncomfortable, know that your journey will take you to being comfortable in what is uncomfortable. You will get through it. Alcoholics Anonymous has a famous saying that starts, "It works if you work it!" I say this to myself all the time because this saying applies to life. The second part is, "So do the work because you are worth it." Remember, to do the work, it takes a village. Seek help and surround yourself with a positive environment.

Living an Intentional Life

Living an intentional life is where you begin to create habits that result in positive living. One thing that has helped me a lot is becoming a Leadership Coach. Besides my master's in executive leadership, I earned two different coaching certifications. What is great about being a coach is the focus is on where you are today and where you want to be tomorrow. Life Coaches and the like don't focus on the past; that is the job of a therapist. We focus on challenging your current mindset so that you can reach your full potential and not be held back. This means learning to live intentionally. Staying on point with what you want to accomplish. Identify what may be holding you back and work on ways to move forward. What can you do today to make this day a great day? What can you do tomorrow to set yourself up for a great day? When you create a mindset of intentional living, you move from living with good intentions to living intentionally. A good intention is a desire. Intentional living is action. A good intention is a wish. Intentional living is purpose. A good intention is someday. Intentional living is today. Get the picture? Turn your good intentions into words of intentional living, and the result will be a life that matters—a life free from being controlled by your emotional baggage.

Intentional living is a practice, not a one-time decision. It is day-to-day self-talk about what you want to accomplish despite your baggage. It is establishing small goals that create small wins that have big results overall. To start with, I would find an accountability partner. Whether it is a coach, a friend, or a family member, it should be someone who will hold you accountable and encourage you to live your intention without judging you if you fall short. You may not succeed the first time, but if you persist every day to live intentionally, it will stick. The more you do this, the more you create a great habit of living in your strengths and not what holds you back.

In John Maxwell's book "Intentional Living," he compares the difference between living intentionally and living unintentionally:

- Intentional living always has an idea. Unintentional living always has an excuse.

- Intentional living fixes the situation. Unintentional living fixes the blame.

- Intentional living makes it happen. Unintentional living wonders what happened.

- Intentional living says, "Here is something I can do." Unintentional living says, "Why doesn't someone else do something?"

One thing I did was find a quote or a prayer and mindfully say it to myself every day. Sometimes it was, "It works if you work it," which I said when I felt like giving in or giving up. "Today is a good day for a good day" is what I say to myself to start my day with a positive, forward-thinking attitude. When I find myself frustrated with things I can't control, the Serenity Prayer pushes me out of my baggage zone. The Serenity Prayer, written in the early 1930s by Reinhold Niebuhr and embraced by Alcoholics Anonymous (AA) in the 1940s, is powerful. I can't explain the irony of two of the most common things I say to myself coming from AA. I have not been to an AA meeting, but I have had several encounters with people who turned their lives around by attending AA meetings, many of whom are veterans.

God grant me the serenity to accept the things I cannot change, the courage to change the things I can, and the wisdom to know the difference.

For me, creating a habit of self-talk inspires forward movement. It gets me out of the "woe is me" mindset, which is destructive and a clear trigger that I am living in my emotional baggage. Most importantly, the best talk I have is when I am talking to God.

When I feel my weakest and at a loss as to why I am not moving forward, one song comes to mind. It was a song I learned when I first accepted Christ as my Lord and Savior. Every time I finish the chorus, I have a strength I didn't have before. It is my go-to song:

> *Trust and obey, for there's no other way*
> *To be happy in Jesus, but to trust and obey*
> *And 'Tis so sweet to trust in Jesus*
> *Just to take Him at His Word*
> *Just to rest upon His promise*
> *Just to know "Thus saith the Lord"*
> *Oh, Trust and obey, for there's no other way*
> *To be happy in Jesus, but to trust and obey*

When you intentionally decide to make the transition from baggage to freedom, these are the steps I take. First, decide that you need to let go to move forward. To do that, confront your feelings and face them head-on so you can forgive those in your life who have hurt you or caused trauma. Finally, start your action plan by living intentionally, setting small goals that lead to your vision for your life. Along the way, seek help from people who have figured this out before, like joining a church, a bible study, or if necessary, going back to therapy. This is not a destination; this is a journey. You learn a little and do a little. So let's get to it!

Chapter 6

Emotional Baggage – A Spiritual Journey

"Therefore, if anyone is in Christ, the new creation has come:
The old has gone, the new is here!"
—2 Corinthians 5:17 (NIV)

Emotional baggage, though often unnoticed, profoundly impacts our lives. It affects our relationships, decisions, and overall well-being. In this chapter, I explore how reconciling emotional baggage parallels living a life of faith. Both processes involve forgiveness, surrender, continuous growth, and the courage to move forward. As someone deeply rooted in Christian faith, I share my journey and invite you to reflect on your own path, regardless of your spiritual beliefs.

> Reflect on your own journey: What emotional burdens have you been carrying, and how have they affected your life?

Understanding Emotional Baggage

When emotional baggage encompasses unresolved issues, traumas, and negative experiences that we carry with us. It can manifest as fear, mistrust, or self-doubt, influencing our actions and reactions. Overcoming this baggage is crucial for personal growth and healthier relationships. Just as emotional healing is a continuous process, so is spiritual growth. Both require dedication, introspection, and an open heart.

Reconciling emotional baggage mirrors the journey of faith, involving forgiveness, surrender, and continuous growth. The steps are: FORGIVE – SURRENDER THE BAGGAGE – DO THE WORK TO MOVE FORWARD – EMBRACE YOUR NEW LIFE BAGGAGE FREE – GROW A LITTLE MORE – DO A LITTLE MORE, rinse and repeat. Both reconciling emotional baggage and living a life of active faith in God are continuous journeys. The moment you stop growing on this journey, emotional baggage can creep back in and take control.

> Think about the areas of your life where you might need to forgive, surrender, and grow. How can you begin to apply these steps?

This is not an easy chapter for me to write because I feel some readers may not have a spiritual belief to turn to, or if they do, it may be different from my belief as a Christian. All I ask is that you fear not and have an open mind. We all have crosses to bear, and it is up to us to choose how we overcome the emotional obstacles that hold us back. I cannot imagine how much more destructive my life would have been had I not chosen Jesus as my Savior. Surrendering to something unseen is the hardest thing one can do; yet faith, from a secular point of view, means having complete trust and belief in someone or something. Complete trust and belief— those are mighty big words, and if our faith is broken at this level, what then?

What I have found in my life is that human and self-reliance only go so far. As humans, we are limited to thinking within our box or the box of the person you are seeking help from. We can do a lot of "outward" things to help ourselves, but since emotional baggage lives in our hearts, I highly recommend going where God lives—in our hearts—where God does His best work. It is our hearts that influence our minds, determining our actions. Therefore, the healing process needs to start in our hearts so that we can positively influence our minds, resulting in healthier choices for our lives. The healthier the choices we make, the greater our potential.

> **Reflect on your reliance on yourself or others: Have you been trying to handle your emotional baggage alone? What difference could it make to allow God (or a higher power) into the healing process?**

Faith in God is not much different than the secular meaning of faith; however, the challenge is faith, from a believer's perspective, is the ability to surrender our complete trust and belief in God based on evidence but not total proof. I have often wondered, why is it that many of us require total proof to believe or have faith in God, but when it comes to believing in others, total proof is not necessary? Could it be because our human minds tell us that it is easier to have faith in something or someone we can see? If, like me, you have been living and suffering with your emotional baggage only to find yourself still lost, why not try God on for size? We have no trouble crying out to God in times of need, but what if your cries were based on a relationship with Him and not just an occasional cry for help? God does wonders when you choose to work with Him to build a strong foundation of faith in Him. Otherwise, trust me, it is a crapshoot and can be a roller coaster ride.

> Consider your faith: How has your need for proof impacted your relationship with God? What would it look like to trust in God without needing all the answers first?

Initial Faith Journey

My journey with faith began in childhood, shaped by misunderstandings and fears. Raised in a Catholic environment where much was misunderstood, I associated God with fear and judgment. Church visits were rare, and my early encounters with faith were driven by the fear of punishment rather than a genuine understanding of God's love. Back then, being a Christian meant trying to be a good person and doing good deeds. The phrase "fear God" was literal to me, and my first confession only reinforced this belief. I thought good deeds were a ticket to Heaven, and I feared I would never be good enough.

> Reflect on your early experiences with faith or spirituality:
> How did they shape your understanding of God?

My first confession was terrifying. The rule was that you couldn't receive communion unless you went to confession first. Driven by fear, I even forgot the opening phrase: "Bless me, Father, for I have sinned. My last confession was…". The Priest scolded me, much like I was scolded at home, and I became terrified. I wondered if God was mad at me too. I was left questioning whether I would ever be good enough to go to Heaven.

My siblings and I attended Catholic school for a couple of years, but our experiences were very different. I loved the structure and rules; they gave me a clear understanding of how to stay in good standing both at home and at school. My siblings, on the other hand, liked to test the waters by challenging the rules, making their experience much more difficult. With my limited exposure to church and God, my understanding of Christianity was very basic. I had no concept of being in a relationship with Christ. I just knew I had to follow the rules. I believed I had to earn my Father's love. Whether at home or at church, the theme of "never being good enough" defined my life. This is why I feared God in the same way I feared my father.

Of course, at such a young age I didn't truly understand how fear, good deeds, and God worked. Now, I can confidently say that "fearing God" is more about awe and reverence than the human version of fear. We are in awe because we will never be "good enough" or "do enough" for God – and we're not supposed to. That is the beauty and point of Christianity. It is through grace, not deeds, that brings us to Heaven. If only I had learned that back then. Would I have found a way to feel good enough?

> **Reflect on your current beliefs: Do you feel you have to earn love or approval? How might this belief be influencing your relationship with God or others?**

High School Struggles

So how does this relate to my faith in Christ? During high school, I tried to find outlets to fill the emptiness I felt inside. Gymnastics became my closest friend, offering structure and distraction. However, at the same time, it solidified my I am not good enough baggage. Since I seated third best on the team and not number one, all I could hear was my dad saying, "You're not good enough so you can't be good enough?" I also tried cheerleading and joined the drama club, where I found some solace playing characters that allowed me to escape from reality. Despite these outlets – whether through sports or drama – I still felt incredibly alone, yearning for normalcy and acceptance. None of these activities filled the deeper void within me.

No matter how much I was looking to feel better about myself outwardly, it just wasn't healing me inwardly. Having no idea how my life was about to change, God was calling out to me. I just didn't know it yet. You see, that is how God works. He reaches inward and slowly works His way throughout all of you so you can grow as a person and a Christian. It is not about religion; it is about a relationship, which can only be accomplished one to one: you and God. Everything else, whatever that God given plan is for you, will come in time—God's time. God knew I needed Him before I knew what it meant to have God be a part of my life. I knew I was looking for something, but I made the mistake that most people make when it comes to accepting God in our lives. I wanted God in my life, but the reality is God doesn't want to fit into our lives; He wants us to be a part of His. Trust me, when I say the latter works so much better.

> Reflect on your own search for acceptance: How have you tried to fill the void in your life? What role could God (or spiritual growth) play in filling that void?

Life just kept going along like I wasn't even a part of it. I hated going home, and once gymnastics and the school plays were done, life was non-existent for me until one fateful day. A boy sitting behind me on the bus, tapped me on the shoulder. For almost two years we had been riding the same bus every day, but we had never spoken a word to each other. I didn't even realize he was on the bus until he approached me. That's how isolated I was – so lost in my own world that I only noticed the bullies. I was constantly on edge, afraid of that crowd and focused on avoiding their attention.

Looking back, I still wonder what made him decide to break the silence. It couldn't have been easy to approach someone as withdrawn as I was, someone who had spent years hiding behind the walls I had built to protect myself from being noticed. Yet, for some reason, he took the plunge and introduced himself to me. Maybe he saw something in me that I couldn't see in myself, or maybe he just decided that being strangers after all this time did not make sense, or maybe he was doing God's work. At that time, I didn't have the answer but whatever the reason, that small act of kindness left a lasting impression on me. It was a reminder that even in the depths of my isolation, I wasn't as invisible as I thought, at least not to God.

It was the beginning of a major shift in my life. It was a God thing. I didn't know it then, but God heard my cries and was answering my prayers, even when I didn't know how to pray. This boy, Steve, took the time to get to know me. From this point on, every day he saved me a seat on the bus. Eventually, he invited me to meet several of his friends at a coffee house. There I met the nicest people, and for the first time, I was good enough! I was welcomed, and I felt like I had so much in common with everyone. I found myself surrounded by kids—kids that were happy just to be kids. No drugs, no alcohol, no mischief, no lying, stealing, or cheating; just kids that loved God with confidence and assurance that *"God can do all things for those who love Him according to His will" (Romans 8:28)*. Most of these kids had a strong relationship with God, and those of us who didn't felt like we were exactly where we needed to be. There was music, laughter, and fellowship with kids and some adults making sure everyone had good, clean fun. I was flabbergasted. I had no idea this existed! No one made fun of me. I was no longer ugly, short, or uncool. Being on the outside of a circle, whether at home or at school, no longer existed. When talking about God, it was from a simple, non-threatening but profound perspective, and I wanted to know more.

The music was Christian music, which I had never heard before. It wasn't the rock-n-roll that I all too often heard when I was at home, at volumes that would blow your eardrums out. Christian music was soothing, heartwarming, and touched the very core of me that was pleading for help. In other words, my soul, was being reached for the first time. Up until then, I didn't even know I had a soul, but I knew whatever was burning inside of me had to be released. It was where all my pain lived. It was where all my emotional baggage was being stored.

> **Reflect on how music or other forms of expression have impacted your spiritual journey: How do these moments of connection help you release emotional burdens?**

I spent a lot of time with this Christian youth group and eventually chose to surrender myself to the belief that Christ died for me. *"For God so loved the world that he gave his only begotten son, so that whoever believes in Him will have eternal life"* (John 3:16 NIV). I was saved, and I was counting on Jesus never to let me down, to protect me and move me forward in life. I thought I finally no longer needed my coping skills to survive my home life. Now I had Jesus. Instead of burying myself, I was learning to put on my armor of God. Ephesians 6:11 says, *"Put on the whole armor of God, that you may be able to stand against the wiles of the devil."* There is no doubt in my mind that choosing God saved me from the destruction that was happening at home. When there was no hope, I now had hope. When I couldn't trust and believe in my family, I now had God, and God surrounded me with wonderful people that helped me survive such a troubling atmosphere. For the first time in my life, I felt loved, even though love itself was such a strange emotion for me. Eventually, that boy who tapped me on my shoulder became my boyfriend, and his family showed me a type of family love that I never knew existed. It was genuine, it was encouraging, and it was heartwarming. With the kind of family, I had and all the drama that went with that, they could have easily discouraged their son from dating me, but instead, they embraced me. We went to church every Sunday morning and had lunch at

Friendly's afterward. A time that I cherish to this day. My belief in God was no longer based on fear but replaced with love—God's love for me. As a testament to my faith in Christ, I got baptized on Easter Sunday, 1979. I even volunteered to give my testimony on a televised Youth for Christ telethon with Johnny Cash by my side to help raise money for youth groups all around the country. I was all in with God, and I thought my problems and dysfunctional life were behind me—until they weren't.

> Reflect on your experiences with faith communities: How have these experiences shaped your understanding of love, acceptance, and God's role in your life?

College and Faith Challenges

So, what happened to my emotional baggage? Did God set me free from it? Sadly, not at first, but that's on me, not on Him. Many people have the illusion that once you commit yourself to God, He magically swoops in and saves you from all the burdens that weigh you down. If only it were that easy. Imagine, however, if it was that easy? Would we even have a need for faith?

Becoming a Christian is often a deeply emotional experience at the start, but being a Christian is something else entirely – it's and intentional, lifelong commitment. That's the hard part, which is why faith is often described as the "road less traveled." Just like any relationship, once the honeymoon phase ends, you begin to face both the blessings and the challenges of living in faith. It's in those moments that growth begins, from the inside out, as you build your relationship with God.

I was so focused on believing in Christ that I missed the essential step of nurturing my relationship with God. I was one of those people who just wanted to feel His love and have Him swoop in and fix everything but that is not how it works. Whether you're on a Christian path or another, growth doesn't happen without effort. I believed, but wasn't doing the work to build the foundation that would allow God to transform me within. (It is no surprise to me now that I am a Leadership Development Coach, Speaker, Trainer. First you build the leader within. Then you focus on how you can impact others.)

Consider your own spiritual growth: Have you been seeking quick fixes or a deeper, more sustained relationship with God? What steps can you take to nurture this relationship?

My stumbling blocks showed up when I went to college, but even then, I didn't realize how my decisions were connected to my childhood trauma. The plan was to get away from my home environment as soon as I was able. The decision then was to go to a Christian college where I thought I could earn my degree while being with a group of people whose values and beliefs were aligned with mine. As it turned out, I went from one extreme culture to another; only this time, I was on my own. My boyfriend Steve and his family were not there to help navigate me through it My Christian faith was still very much in the early stages of maturity. I was relying on the emotional high of being a Christian, not the foundation that should have been building. I expected to feel safe and loved in this environment and to my dismay, I got the very opposite. I couldn't pass the Bible courses because up until college, I barely read the Bible, let alone memorized the entire thing. The worse I did in college, the more I felt Steve, and his family were too good for me. My emotional baggage was beginning to rear its ugly head.

> **Reflect on your expectations versus reality in life changes: How have past experiences shaped your expectations, and how have you handled the disconnect between expectation and reality?**

Once again, I found myself alone, failing miserably, with no one who understood me. I was confused. I thought Christians had high moral character, but that is not what I was seeing. I forgot that Christians are still human and face the same challenges as everyone else. Sadly, this type of scenario happens all too often and deters people's faith in God. It did mine. Everything seemed upside down! Boys were liking me for the first time, and I found myself just wanting to belong in a world I didn't understand. In a panic, I broke up with Steve, thinking I wanted more. I did exactly what I did as a child: I retreated. I no longer trusted my environment. In a world with many rules, these rules didn't make sense—no smoking, no drinking, no playing card games, no going to secular movies, no dancing. No dancing! I couldn't understand why these behaviors were such a problem for Christians. I spent my entire childhood not doing what my siblings did, so those rules weren't temptations for me, but apparently, they were for a lot of the students attending that college. I wondered what these students and faculty were afraid of—life? Was this the part of God I gave my life to? Stop the train! I have to get off! I was retreating. Time to find another safe place.

Reflect on your own retreats: When have you felt the need to retreat from an environment or situation? How did you cope, and what could you do differently now?

After two years of trying and failing both socially and scholastically, I dropped out of college and found myself in an environment that was like my siblings'. After all, I knew how to survive that life better than I understood the so-called Christian environment. Don't get me wrong, my belief in God never wavered, but my understanding of how to live with or for God apparently had a long way to go. As I stated before, without understanding and growth, your baggage will once again become your safe place. I was hanging out at bars and testing that way of life. I met a guy four years older than me who seemed to accept and treat me better than the boys in college. It didn't take long before I found myself doing what I swore I would never do, even before I became a Christian—live with a man and all that goes with that. Of course, after about a year, I realized that his drunkenness and drug usage were not the life I was meant to have. It was a gut instinct. Actually, it was God taking care of me in spite of my lack of understanding. Still not realizing that the wash -rinse-repeat nature of my life was filling up my emotional baggage. Every decision was like adding more dirty clothes to an already filled piece of luggage.

Consider the patterns in your life: What patterns of behavior or decision making do you recognize? How have these patterns contributed to your emotional baggage?

In my heart, I think I was hoping God would save me, and He did, but not in a way that I saw or wanted Him to. You see, as much as I believed in God, I still wanted Him to bow to my wants, my desires, my solutions. Because of this, I never seemed to recover—just recoup my losses and start over again. I was constantly negotiating with God, but in reality, I was negotiating with myself so I could fit my choices into what I believed God would be okay with. This is a very vicious cycle to stay in. It is like being in a traffic circle that you can never exit out of. Thankfully, God does not give up on us. The beauty of surrendering your life to Christ is that even when you fall—and you will fall—God is there. He will protect you. He will also challenge you, and when He does, that is Him calling you to come to Him, to rely on Him, and to trust Him. That's faith, and your faith is limited by your growth as a Christian, much like your belief in yourself is limited by the baggage you carry. That is the connection.

> **Reflect on your relationship with God: How have your desires or expectations shaped your faith journey? What would it look like to fully surrender and trust in God's plan?**

Reconciling with Faith

When we reach our "aha" moment and choose to reconcile our baggage, we must understand that this process is not a quick fix – just as becoming a believer is not a quick and easy journey. Neither is the choice of becoming a believer in Christ. In fact, the choice is much easier than the process, and I wouldn't have it any other way. It is foolish to think that we can unravel and reconcile years of hurt, pain, and dysfunction in the same instance we decide to unload the baggage. This is why my belief in Christ is the key ingredient to laying down my baggage. If I just relied on myself to pick up the pieces of my emotional baggage, then eventually, I would have found this task to be daunting and impossible. Hope and possibility would have been buried so far in my baggage that I couldn't find them. But with Jesus, hope and possibility are ALWAYS reachable.

Consider where your hope and possibility lie: Have you been relying solely on your own strength, or have you invited God into the process?

How might your journey change if you did?

Like my school years, I was not a quick learner when it came to the understanding of being in a relationship with God. Today, the phrase "lean not on my own understanding" has a whole new meaning to me. Many years and many decisions based on my emotional baggage were rooted in me leaning on my own understanding, which meant that God couldn't do the work He had in store for me if I didn't let Him in. While His love for me is unconditional, He gives us room to make mistakes so that we can build our faith in Him. Only then can we begin to lean on His understanding.

The beauty of having faith in Jesus is that I don't have to strive for perfection, which is something I always did as a child to gain acceptance or prove myself worthy. I just need to strive for Jesus. The pain associated with reconciling baggage can be shared and given to God. With God, you see that there is a light at the end of the tunnel, and regardless of how long that train ride is, the light and protection of God are always there—even when you think the train has derailed. God will make sure you survive and get back on the track. You just need to always remember to lean on His understanding.

> **Reflect on the perfectionism in your life: Have you been striving for perfection in a way that hinders your growth? How can you shift your focus to striving for a deeper relationship with Jesus instead?**

So if you have read this far, I want to thank you for your open mind. If you struggle with believing in God, here are a few things to think about. For every choice we make in life, there are many perspectives that help us make that choice. Every truth can be perceived as a lie or falsehood. What is right can be wrong in someone else's eyes. So, when someone says that God or believing in God is false, or that Jesus wasn't the son of God, does it mean their statement is true? Of course not. That is that person's choice. When lies are spoken, and enough people speak those lies, does that make the lie true? Of course not. That is their choice. When someone says, "I can steal from my brother because he stole from me," does that make stealing from my brother right? Of course, not—stealing is stealing, and two wrongs don't make a right.

So, when someone says that God is your salvation, Proverbs 3: 5 6 (NIV) says, *"Trust in the LORD with all your heart and lean not on your own understanding; in all your ways submit to him, and he will make your paths straight."* Would you believe them? The beauty is that it is your choice, and Jesus wants you to make that choice one way or another. I choose Christ because not choosing Him seemed to have dire consequences that I wasn't sure I could overcome on my own. I choose Christ because He is the one constant in life. People are not perfect, and many times cannot meet your needs when you need them to, or they may not have the right words or the right nurturing capability to get you through your next piece of baggage. But Christ was sent to this earth to overcome your pain, and His spirit is inside your heart, ready to relieve you of your baggage.

> **Consider your choices: What has kept you from fully choosing to trust in God? How might your life change if you took that step today?**

To say no to Christ seemed to me to be like saying no to hope. To say no to Christ seemed to me like saying no to what is possible. Even if you are unsure about your belief in God, believe in the possibility that God is your salvation and journey toward freeing yourself of emotional baggage. Mark 9:23 says, *"Anything is possible for the one who believes."* Giving God the benefit of truth, even while some doubt may lie in your heart where all your emotional baggage lives, reminds me of the parable of the mustard seed in the Gospel of Matthew. This powerful metaphor originates from the remarkable transformation of a small mustard seed into a robust and steadfast tree. The mustard seed symbolizes growth, dependence, and faith. In other words, even with some doubt, it only takes a small sense of belief to believe. Matthew 17:20 says, *"For truly I say to you, if you have faith like a grain of mustard seed... nothing will be impossible for you."* Jesus wanted to highlight that it does not take much faith for God to work in a person much like me and maybe you. Belief in God is within all of us. It is just a matter of choice. Think about letting God lead the way in your journey to let go of the emotional baggage that has kept you from reaching the full potential God has prepared for you. The enemy of emotional baggage is vulnerability. Iin my experience, people often struggle to believe in God because they're afraid to be vulnerable. Vulnerability means putting yourself out there, even when there's a risk of getting hurt. It's essential to allow ourselves to be vulnerable- healing cannot happen without it.

> **Reflect on the mustard seed: What small steps of faith can you take today to begin your journey of letting go and trusting God?**

Chapter 7

Strategies for Overcoming Emotional Baggage

"Brothers and sisters, I do not consider myself yet to have taken hold of it. But one thing I do: Forgetting what is behind and straining toward what is ahead, I press on toward the goal to win the prize for which God has called me heavenward in Christ Jesus."
—*Philippians 3:13-14 (NIV)*

When it comes to overcoming emotional baggage, Philippians 3:13 14 resonates deeply with me. The message is simple yet profound: to move forward, we must let go of the past. The journey of reconciling emotional baggage is ongoing, much like the pursuit of happiness. Being free from the emotional burdens that hold you back is not a one-time achievement; it requires continual nurturing and healing so that the triggers and limiting beliefs associated with emotional baggage no longer own you.

Overcoming emotional baggage is not a linear process. It involves ups and downs, moments of clarity, and times of doubt. It's like peeling an onion—each layer you peel away reveals another, deeper layer that needs to be addressed. The key is to be patient with yourself and understand that healing is a journey, not a destination. This perspective is crucial because it removes the pressure to "arrive" at a state of perfect emotional health and instead encourages continual growth and learning.

Imagine what your life could look like if you unburdened yourself from your emotional baggage. What would change? How would you feel? These are not just hypothetical questions; they are the starting points for creating a vision for your future. When stuck in your emotional baggage, creating this vision can feel daunting. Yet it is essential to focus on what excites and energizes you. Dream big—allow yourself to envision greatness without limitations. Whether you are young or old, your life is a blank canvas, and you are the artist.

One of the most powerful exercises you can do is to close your eyes and visualize your life free from emotional baggage. What does that look like? Perhaps you see yourself more confident, pursuing dreams you once thought were out of reach, or simply feeling at peace with yourself and your past. Visualization is not just about daydreaming; it's about creating a mental image of your goals, which can then guide your actions and decisions.

After you've created this vision, write it down. This act of writing crystallizes your thoughts and makes your goals feel more tangible. Include in your writing how fulfilling your dream will align with your purpose in life and who else might benefit from the best version of yourself. This is the beginning of how you can impact your world and those around you. The more detailed your vision, the clearer your path forward will be. Consider what steps you need to take to make this vision a reality. What resources do you need? What changes do you need to make in your daily life?

Strategy One: Seek Help

The path to overcoming emotional baggage is not one to walk alone. Seeking help can take many forms—a therapist, a coach, a mentor, or simply someone you trust to hold you accountable. It's important to recognize that the most successful individuals, whether in personal or professional spheres, understand that they cannot achieve their goals alone. Interestingly enough, we spend most of our childhood and college years seeking help, but as adults, we often view asking for help as a sign of weakness or failure when in fact it is a crucial step toward growth and healing.

> Reflect on your support system: Who can you reach out to for help on your journey? If you feel hesitant, consider what is holding you back and how you can overcome that hesitation.

Often the barriers to seeking help are rooted in fear—fear of judgment, fear of vulnerability, or fear of the unknown. But remember, seeking help is a sign of strength, not weakness. It shows that you are committed to your growth and willing to do what it takes to overcome your challenges.

Depending on the severity of your emotional baggage, the type of help you seek—whether it be a therapist, coach, or mentor—can make a significant difference. Understanding the roles each can play will help you make an informed decision on the best path for you.

Therapists are licensed professionals trained to help you explore your past and understand how it impacts your present. They are particularly helpful if your emotional baggage stems from trauma or deeply ingrained patterns that are difficult to break on your own. Therapy provides a safe space to explore your emotions, gain insights, and develop strategies for managing your feelings and behaviors.

Coaches start with where you are today and move toward your future, helping you to set goals and create a plan to achieve them. They work with you to overcome obstacles and hold you accountable to your commitments. Coaching is particularly effective if you have a clear vision of where you want to go but need guidance on how to get there.

Mentors offer advice and support based on their own experiences. They can provide valuable insights and guidance, particularly if you are navigating a career or personal path that they have already walked. Mentorship is about learning from someone who has been in your shoes and can offer wisdom and perspective.

In my journey, I utilized a combination of all three. Therapy provided me with awareness of my past and how it was affecting my present. It helped me to understand the root causes of my emotional baggage, identify my triggers and limit beliefs and to develop strategies for coping with it. Mentorship, particularly in my professional life, surrounded me with successful individuals who shared my core values. These mentors not only provided guidance but also inspired me to believe in my potential. The process of becoming a certified Leadership Coach gave me the opportunity to combine all my resources, putting a period on my past, living in the present while helping me to define and pursue my goals. Each step along the way reinforced the idea that forgiveness, especially of oneself, is essential in reconciling the past and changing the present.

Consider which type of support resonates most with you. Is it the deep, past focused work of therapy? The goal oriented, future focused approach of coaching? Or the experiential wisdom of a mentor? Each offers unique benefits, and the right choice depends on where you are in your journey and what you hope to achieve.

Strategy Two: Forgiveness

Forgiveness is one of the greatest gifts you can give, whether to yourself or others. It involves an intentional decision to let go of resentment and anger, and its benefits are profound—healthier relationships, improved mental health, and even physical benefits like lower blood pressure and a stronger immune system. Forgiveness is not about condoning the actions that hurt you, nor is it about forgetting what happened. Instead, it is about freeing yourself from the hold that past hurts have on you, allowing you to move forward without the weight of bitterness or regret.

> Reflect on the role of forgiveness in your life: What does forgiveness mean to you? Is there someone you need to forgive, or do you need to forgive yourself?

How would forgiveness change your current state of mind? These are not easy questions to answer, and the process of forgiveness can be challenging. But it is also deeply liberating. Holding on to anger and resentment keeps you tethered to the past, preventing you from fully embracing the present and the future.

For me, forgiveness began with my father. After years of estrangement, we reconnected, and I asked him why he had been so angry all the time. His story was enlightening and seemed to make sense to me, and while it didn't excuse his behavior, it allowed me to understand and ultimately forgive him. You see, his answer made it clear that his hate and anger toward our family wasn't about me or my siblings. It was about his own regrets and bad decisions that led to a life and family he never wanted with my mom. This process wasn't about absolving him of responsibility – it was about freeing myself from the burden of anger and blame. Forgiving him didn't mean that I condoned his actions or that I forgot the pain he caused. Instead, it meant that I chose not to let that pain define me or dictate my future.

Forgiveness doesn't mean forgetting, but it does mean releasing the hold that past hurts have on you. It's about emptying the "box" where you store unresolved pain, so it no longer impacts your present relationships and decisions. The journey of forgiveness can be difficult, but it is vital for emotional healing and growth.

Consider how forgiveness, both of yourself and others, can open the door to new possibilities in your life. It allows you to let go of the past and move forward with a lighter heart and a clearer mind. Forgiveness is not about letting others off the hook; it's about setting yourself free. It can also free you to support those you've forgiven or help others who have experienced the same pain.

Strategy Three: Practice Self Care

Practicing self-care is crucial when overcoming emotional baggage, as it touches every area of your life—mental, physical, environmental, financial, social, recreational, and spiritual. Emotional baggage is isolating, separating you from what you love and the people you care about. Therefore, it is essential to prioritize self-care to reconnect with yourself and the world around you.

> **Reflect on your current self-care practices: Which areas do you currently neglect? How does this neglect impact your overall well-being?**

What steps can you take today to start prioritizing your self-care? Mental self-care is about nourishing your mind, stimulating it, and protecting it from negative influences. This could involve learning new skills, practicing mindfulness, or simply taking time to relax and unwind. It's also about setting boundaries to protect your mental space from unnecessary stress. One powerful practice is journaling, which allows you to process your thoughts and emotions, gain clarity, and reflect on your growth.

Physical self-care includes taking care of your body through exercise, nutrition, and rest. It's about treating your body with the respect it deserves, recognizing that a healthy body supports a healthy mind. Regular exercise, even something as simple as walking, can have a profound impact on your mood and energy levels. If you're not someone who enjoys exercise, don't let it intimidate you. Exercise comes in many forms, and it's okay to start small. Begin with a 15-minute walk and gradually work your way up to adding more time. If you tend to procrastinate, create a to-do list and put exercise at the top. Choose a specific time and stick to it. The more you do this, the less overwhelming it will feel, and soon it will become a habit you enjoy. Plus, there's something incredibly satisfying and motivating about checking that box off your list! You may also find that with the small successes with exercise, eating healthier and getting better sleep are added benefits making your physical care more well-rounded.

Environmental self-care involves creating a living and working space that supports your well-being. This could mean decluttering your home, bringing in more natural light, or creating a dedicated space for relaxation or meditation. Your environment has a significant impact on your mood and productivity, so it's important to make it a space that inspires and uplifts you. I remember when I first bought the house I live in now. I was finally able to have a designated workspace. I made it a point to make that office an extension of me. Sometimes it's not about the "office space" but space in general. It can be as simple as just changing throw pillows.

Financial self-care is about managing your money in a way that reduces stress and supports your goals. This could involve budgeting, saving, investing, or seeking financial advice. Money is often a source of anxiety, but taking control of your finances can give you a sense of empowerment and security. Remember the old saying, "Money doesn't buy happiness."? It's important to recognize when you might start believing otherwise. For a long time, I lived in fear of not having enough money. When my dad left, my mom didn't know how to manage finances and, we quickly became dirt poor. To add to this, she said my dad never paid child support which is why were so poor. (Twelve years later, that story will prove to not be true.). My goal was to never let this happen to me, so money became my focus.

In my current marriage, I recharged my life and became the breadwinner of our household. My husband, who had sold his business three years earlier, was now making a modest income, while my career was at its financial peak. For the first time, I was able to buy a home soley based on my earnings and credit. I was financially independent; something I had never been able to accomplish. I was so proud of myself. Still, I kept wanting more – materially, I craved more. Once you get on that train, it's hard to get off, unless you are forced off. That's exactly what happened.

The company I worked for had its first layoff, and I was on the list. I went from being the breadwinner to having crumbs, but after reviewing our finances, my husband and I realized we would be okay. I thought I'd have to sacrifice my lifestyle, but then it hit me – my lifestyle wasn't what brought me happiness. In the end, when you're not drowning in credit card debt, you'd be surprised how manageable life is with less money. You also learn to redirect your pursuit of happiness. It's within you and not money is required.

Social and recreational self-care are about nurturing your relationships and engaging in activities that bring you joy. It's important to surround yourself with people who uplift and support you and to make time for hobbies and activities that you enjoy. This could mean joining a club, taking up a new hobby, or simply spending time with loved ones. The point is, humans aren't meant to be alone. If the community you're in is catabolic and draining, it's essential t change it as soon as possible. Serving others is one of the best ways to nurture your social and recreational self-care. I had always wanted to serve within the church I was attending, but I didn't know where I fit in. Recently, I finally became a member of that church because I knew it was time. I was tired of looking in from the outside and realized the only thing holding me back was procrastination. The longer I delayed, the more disconnected I felt.

I eventually found my place serving on the production team and I not only enjoy it, but I am also having a blast doing it. More importantly, the more I engage with the community, the more I build trust and credibility, which strengthened my faith and my ability to trust others. Serving others enriches you and the person or people you are serving. If you find yourself spending too much time watching TV or feeling isolated, I encourage you to get out to the house. Maybe go to church. Just get up and get out.

Spiritual self-care involves nurturing your soul, whether through God, religion, meditation, or other practices that connect you with your inner self and the larger universe. For me, spiritual self-care comes from my faith in Jesus. This provides strength, guidance, and a sense of purpose. Whatever your beliefs, it is essential to make time for practices that nourish our spirit and align you with your higher purpose. Just as we need others for social and recreational health, we are not meant to believe and worship alone. Finding the right church is crucial for spiritual growth.

If you believe in God but don't go to church, I encourage you to give it another try. No church is perfect so stop searching for the perfect one. We all have stories of bad experiences in church – I know I do. But if I judged people solely for their mistakes, I'd be left alone: untrusting, angry, cynical, and the list goes on. The same holds true for churches. Instead of focusing on the flaws, try to see the good that church can bring to the community – or better yet, the good you can bring to that church. Visit different churches and find one that resonates with your soul, captures your attention, and offers opportunities for you to contribute.

I was once that person who believed but didn't go to church. I didn't ready my Bible or learn anything about the historical value of scripture either. But growth doesn't happen in isolation. We need like-minded people to hold us accountable, share in our joy and faith, and comfort us in times of doubt. Joining a women's Bible study at my church was uncomfortable for me at first. I was judgmental – I assumed women would be too "churchy". You know the kind I'm talking about. But what I experienced was completely different. Not only am I building a community, but I'm also growing spiritually and gaining a deeper understanding of the Bible.

Side note: Did you know the Bible speaks about some amazing, strong women? I challenge you to look up the story of Esther – a smart, strong, strategic woman who was willing to sacrifice herself for her people. Once I learned about Ester, I started to see the role of women in the Bible differently. I had always assumed the Bible portrayed women as submissive, but it's quite the opposite. If I hadn't made growing my faith intentional, I would have never understood the true strength of woman.

> Consider how these areas intertwine: How does focusing on one area of self-care impact the others? For example, improving your physical health can boost your mental clarity and energy levels, which in turn can enhance your productivity and mood.

How can you create a balanced self-care plan that addresses all aspects of your life? Reflect on the journey of knowing yourself: To grow, you must understand who you are—your strengths, weaknesses, interests, and opportunities. In business they call this the SWOT analysis (strengths, weakness, opportunities and threat.)

When I speak or train people on Leadership, I use the analogy and ask them to consider themselves a business (i.e. Fausta C Phelan, Inc.) and they are the CEO. What would the CEO do to invest and grow their business or are they willing to let their business go out of business. Often times my best decisions is when I step outside of myself and see myself from a 30,000 foot view. I can see things from several perspectives thus making better decisions. This self-awareness will guide you toward healing and growth, helping you reconcile your emotional baggage and move forward. Knowing yourself means being honest about where you are, where you want to go, and what you need to do to get there.

In John Maxwell's book *15 Invaluable Laws of Growth*, the second law is the Law of Awareness—"*You must know yourself to grow yourself.*" This law is a great summary of the strategies recommended above. Putting these strategies into practice puts you on the road to knowing yourself so you can not only grow but also make tremendous strides in reconciling your emotional baggage.

Remember, growth is a continuous journey. It's about taking one step at a time, learning from each experience, and constantly striving to become the best version of yourself. As you navigate through the strategies mentioned in this chapter, keep in mind that the journey is just as important as the destination. Be patient with yourself, celebrate your progress, and stay committed to your growth.

Chapter 8

From Baggage to Purpose

"The purposes of a person's heart are deep waters,
but one who has insight draws them out."
—Proverbs 20:5 (NIV)

The Search for Meaning

Have you ever wrestled with the question, "What is the meaning of life?" This question has been the cornerstone of philosophical and spiritual inquiry for centuries, and it's one that every individual must confront at some point in their life. However, a more pressing and personal question might be, "What is the meaning of *my* life?" This query often arises during times of crisis, transition, or when we are faced with the consequences of decisions shaped by our emotional baggage.

The pursuit of this answer can feel overwhelming, particularly when our past experiences, mistakes, and unresolved emotions cloud our judgment. It's easy to fall into a cycle of regret, asking questions like, "What else do I have to deal with?" or "When will my life finally turn around?" These questions are steeped in a victim mentality, which keeps us anchored in the past. But to discover your true purpose, you must adopt a forward-thinking approach. This means shifting your focus from surviving the past to thriving in the present and future. Be intentional with your mindset so it becomes a habit. When you catch yourself slipping into a victim mentality, take a moment to pause, breathe, and reflect on your thoughts. Are they feeding you negativity, or are they helping you see opportunities in an otherwise challenging situation.

Shifting from Victim to Victor: A Personal Journey

Let me share a personal story that illustrates this shift from victimhood to victory. During the preparation for this book, I revisited some of my most painful memories—memories that had long been buried but continued to influence my life in subtle, insidious ways. One such memory involved my first marriage to Klaus, a relationship that was fraught with challenges but also brought my daughter into the world.

For years, I struggled with deep regret over that marriage. It was a relationship that drained me emotionally and left me in a precarious financial situation. Yet, I couldn't bring myself to fully regret it because it gave me my daughter, the light of my life. This internal conflict—a mix of remorse, sadness, and unresolved pain—was a reflection of the emotional baggage I carried.

The marriage itself was a mistake, but the child it produced was a blessing. This dichotomy is something many people experience; we often find ourselves trapped between the regret of a past decision and the love for something or someone that resulted from it. For years, I tried to reconcile these conflicting emotions, but it wasn't until I began to focus on my purpose—helping others avoid the mistakes I made—that I found peace.

When I reflect on this time in my life, I realize that my actions were driven by fear, insecurity, and a lack of purpose. I moved from one relationship to another, searching for stability and meaning, but all I found was more pain. It wasn't until I began to understand and reconcile my emotional baggage that I could see the broader purpose behind my experiences. I realized that my purpose wasn't just about surviving; it was about using my story to help others navigate their own struggles.

This realization didn't happen overnight. It took years of introspection, therapy, and spiritual growth. I had to confront the darkest parts of my past, forgive myself for my mistakes, and learn to see those experiences as opportunities for growth rather than failures. This shift in perspective was transformative—it allowed me to move from a place of victimhood to a position of empowerment.

The Role of Emotional Baggage in Finding Purpose

When you are caught up in your unreconciled baggage, finding your purpose can be incredibly challenging. Emotional baggage clouds your judgment, filling your mind with limiting beliefs and triggers that convince you that you're not worthy of success or happiness. These beliefs act as invisible chains, holding you back from pursuing your true potential.

One of the most insidious effects of emotional baggage is that it keeps you trapped in a cycle of negative thinking. You start to believe that you don't deserve a better life, that you're incapable of change, or that your past mistakes have permanently damaged your future. These thoughts are powerful—they shape your reality and dictate your actions. If you believe you are unworthy, you will unconsciously sabotage your efforts to improve your life. This is why reconciling your emotional baggage is so critical to finding your purpose.

The concept of limiting beliefs is central to understanding how emotional baggage affects our lives. Limiting beliefs are the deeply ingrained thoughts and assumptions that hold us back. They can take many forms: "I'm not smart enough," "I'm too old to change," "I'm not deserving of love," or "I'll never be successful." These beliefs often stem from past experiences—perhaps you were told as a child that you would never amount to anything, or maybe you've internalized societal messages that suggest certain opportunities are out of reach for people like you.

To uncover and challenge these limiting beliefs, it's essential to engage in deep self-reflection. Ask yourself: What beliefs do I hold about myself that might be holding me back? Where did these beliefs come from? Are they really true, or have I accepted them without question? This process can be uncomfortable as it forces you to confront painful memories and acknowledge the ways in which you have allowed your past to dictate your present. However, it's a necessary step toward freeing yourself from the chains of emotional baggage.

The Misconception of Happiness as Purpose

One of the biggest misconceptions about purpose is that it's synonymous with happiness. Many people believe that once they achieve happiness, they will have found their purpose. However, the opposite is true purpose creates happiness, not the other way around. If your pursuit of happiness is based on acquiring material possessions or achieving superficial goals, it will always leave you feeling unfulfilled. True happiness stems from living a life of purpose, a life that is focused on serving others and making a positive impact in the world.

I too fell into this trap. For years, I believed that if I could achieve financial independence, find the perfect job, and settle down with the right partner, I would finally be happy. But even after I accomplished these goals, I still felt something was missing. It wasn't until I started focusing on my God given passions, talents, and values that I discovered what was truly missing, purpose?

This realization came with a profound shift in my priorities. I began to understand that happiness is a byproduct of living a life aligned with my purpose. When you are living in alignment with your purpose, even the challenges and hardships you face take on a different meaning. They become opportunities for growth rather than obstacles to happiness.

Consider the story of Viktor Frankl, a Holocaust survivor and psychiatrist who wrote about his experiences in the concentration camps in his book *Man's Search for Meaning*. Frankl observed that those who survived the horrors of the camps were not necessarily the strongest or the healthiest, but those who had a sense of purpose—a reason to live. He famously said, "Those who have a 'why' to live can bear with almost any 'how'." Frankl's insights highlight the profound power of purpose in shaping our lives and our ability to endure suffering.

Defining Purpose in Your Life

Defining your life's purpose can be daunting, especially when you're surrounded by misconceptions about what purpose really is. Let's start by clarifying what purpose is not. Purpose is not simply setting a goal, although goals can help you achieve your purpose. It is not the pursuit of happiness, nor is it self-focused. Purpose is about contributing to something greater than yourself. It's about using your unique gifts to serve others and make a positive impact in the world.

Purpose has been defined by many authors and thought leaders in various ways, but one common thread runs through all their definitions: purpose is about serving others. Jill Suttie, in her article "Seven Ways to Find Purpose In Your Life" (Greater Good Magazine, August 6, 2020), states that "purpose is all about applying your skills toward contributing to the greater good in a way that matters to you." Similarly, Kevin Cashman, in his book *Leadership From the Inside Out* (Berrett Koehler Publishers, San Francisco, CA, 2008), describes purpose as "the flow of life through us as it serves all those it touches." Rick Warren, in *The Purpose Driven Life* (Zondervan, Grand Rapids, MI, 2002), emphasizes that purpose is rooted in our relationship with God and our contributions to His kingdom.

One of the most powerful ways to begin defining your purpose is to engage in self-reflection. This process requires honesty and vulnerability, as it involves examining your deepest desires, values, and motivations. Start by asking yourself: What are the things that truly matter to me? What activities or causes make me feel most alive? What strengths and talents do I have that can be used to serve others? These questions can help you uncover the core elements of your purpose. Notice these questions are forward thinking. This is intentional because forward-thinking questions focus on your strengths. Now, imagine the despair that would come if you flipped those questions to negatives. It's important to stay away from negative thinking. These questions also help you discover your "why". You may recognize this concept from leadership coaching or motivational training, where finding your "why" is the key to unlocking your purpose.

For example: I wanted to write a book about overcoming emotional baggage. Why? Because if I can help people reconcile their emotional baggage earlier in their lives, it will positively impact not only their present lives but also the lives of those connected to them and will be connected to them in the future – like children.

Another helpful exercise is to think about the legacy you want to leave behind. Imagine yourself at the end of your life, looking back on the years you've lived. What do you want to be remembered for? What impact do you want to have made on the world? These reflections can provide valuable insights into your purpose and guide you in making decisions that align with your long-term goals.

The Role of Passion in Purpose

Passion plays a crucial role in defining and living your purpose. Passion is the fuel that drives you to pursue your goals with enthusiasm and determination. It's what makes the hard work feel worthwhile and the setbacks feel temporary. Without passion, it's easy to lose motivation and give up when challenges arise.

To identify your passions, think about the activities or causes that make you feel most energized and fulfilled. What do you love doing so much that you lose track of time? What topics or issues are you most passionate about? These passions are not random—they are clues to your purpose.

However, it's important to distinguish between fleeting passions and those that are deeply rooted in your values and identity. Not every interest or hobby is meant to be part of your purpose. Some passions may serve as hobbies or ways to relax, while others may be integral to your life's mission. To determine whether a passion is aligned with your purpose, ask yourself: Does this passion contribute to my long-term goals? Does it align with my values and the impact I want to make in the world?

It's also important to recognize that passions can evolve over time. What you're passionate about in your twenties may be different from what drives you in your forties or sixties. This is a natural part of growth and self-discovery. As you gain new experiences and insights, your understanding of your purpose may deepen and expand. The key is to remain open to this evolution and to allow your passions to guide you on your journey.

The Intersection of Talents, Values, and Purpose

Purpose is not just about passion—it's also about leveraging your unique talents and aligning them with your values. Your talents are the skills and abilities that come naturally to you, the things you excel at with little effort. These talents are not random; they are gifts that have been given to you for a reason. When you use your talents in service of others, you are living your purpose.

However, talents alone are not enough. They must be aligned with your values—the principles and beliefs that guide your actions and decisions. Your values are the compass that directs your life, helping you stay true to your purpose even when the path is difficult. When your talents and values are in sync, you are able to make a meaningful impact in the world.

To identify your values, think about the principles that are most important to you. What do you stand for? What do you believe in? What are the non-negotiables in your life? These values will help you make decisions that are aligned with your purpose and keep you on track even when faced with challenges.

It's also important to recognize that your values may change over time as you grow and evolve. This is a natural part of the journey, and it's essential to regularly revisit your values to ensure they are still in alignment with your purpose. By staying true to your values, you can live a life that is authentic and fulfilling.

Steps to Finding Your Purpose

Now that you've begun to explore what your purpose might be, let's look at some practical steps to help you fully discover and live that purpose. These steps are crucial not only for identifying your purpose but also for keeping your emotional baggage at bay.

1. **Discover What Is Important to You:** John Maxwell once said, "There are two great days in your life: the day you were born and the day you discover why." Your values are the direction signs that lead you to your purpose. They are what give meaning to your life. To discover what is truly important to you, reflect on the times in your life when you felt most energized and fulfilled. What were you doing? Who were you with? What values were you honoring during those times?

2. **Turn Your Past Experiences into Triumphs:** We all have a story, and for many of us, that story includes trauma and hardship. But instead of letting those experiences define you, use them to fuel your purpose. Your past experiences, both good and bad, have shaped who you are today. By turning those experiences into a positive force, you can help others who may be going through similar struggles. This is how you turn lemons into lemonade—by using your pain as a catalyst for growth and service.

3. **Work Within Your Talents and Strengths:** We all have strengths and talents that have been given to us for a reason. These gifts are clues to our purpose. When you put your strengths into action, your purpose becomes clearer and easier to live by. If you're unsure of what your strengths are, consider taking a personality assessment or asking those who know you well for their input. Often, others can see our strengths more clearly than we can. If you've taken a personality test such as Maxwell's DISC, ask yourself these questions: Where is it now? When was the last time you reviewed or applied it to your home or work life? Are you the same person now as you were when you took the test? Has your environment changed since then? Just like you schedule regular maintenance for your car, you should also schedule regular maintenance for yourself.

4. **Volunteer and Serve Others:** Volunteering is a powerful way to discover and live your purpose. When you volunteer, you shift your focus from yourself to others, which is the essence of living a purposeful life. It's not about finding the perfect volunteer opportunity; it's about taking action and

serving in whatever capacity you can. Start small and be open to trying different things. The experience that excites you the most could be the key to unlocking your purpose. If you're a parent, I encourage you to involve your children in volunteering as early as possible. This is where character, humility, integrity, and selflessness are developed. Plus, it doesn't hurt that it can keep them off the computer. I think I waited too long, but when my daughter was in high school, I had her volunteer at the local fire department. It taught her all of the above, as well as the importance of being a strong woman in a male dominated environment. Stay focused on your course, keep your eye on your purpose, and you will exceed your expectations.

5. **Embrace Continuous Learning and Growth**: Finding your purpose is not a one-time event; it's a lifelong journey of self-discovery and growth. This means being open to new experiences, learning from your mistakes, and continually refining your understanding of your purpose. It's important to approach life with a growth mindset, seeing challenges and setbacks as opportunities for learning rather than as failures.

6. **Build a Support System**: Surround yourself with people who support your purpose and encourage your growth. This could be a mentor, a coach, a spiritual advisor, or a group of likeminded individuals who share your values. Having a strong support system can provide you with the guidance, encouragement, and accountability you need to stay on track and continue growing. I remembered how impactful this was in my life. As a teenager, I surrounded

myself with adults who had qualities I admired and aspired to develop. I did the same for my daughter. When I had to work and leave her with sitters or friends, I made sure they were people who embodied the characteristics I wanted her to learn. One of my friends was an artist, and now Brittney is a talented artist herself with a knack for creativity. Her canvas is her camera and the paper she writes her scripts on. Another friend was strong and self-reliant, teaching Brittney practical skills to take care of herself. Today, she's is very successful not just because of me, although I would like to give myself all the credit, but the community I surrounded her in. As parents, we can't always be everywhere at once, so it's important to choose caregivers wisely, making sure they don't just "watch" your kids, but make sure they can positively influence your child's growth

7. **Stay Aligned with Your Purpose**: Once you've identified your purpose, it's important to stay aligned with it in your daily actions and decisions. This means regularly checking in with yourself to ensure that you are living in accordance with your values and making choices that support your long term goals. It also means being willing to make changes, when necessary, whether that's adjusting your goals, changing your environment, or letting go of relationships that no longer serve your purpose.

8. **Reflect on Your Journey**: Take time to regularly reflect on your journey and the progress you've made. This could be through journaling, meditation, or simply taking a walk in nature. Reflection allows you to gain insights into your experiences, celebrate your successes, and learn from your

challenges. It also helps you stay connected to your purpose and keep your goals in perspective.

These steps are not a one size fits all solution, but they provide a framework for discovering and living your purpose. The important thing is to stay committed to the journey and to be patient with yourself as you grow and evolve.

The Role of Faith in Purpose

For many people, faith plays a central role in understanding and living their purpose. Faith provides a sense of meaning and direction, offering guidance and comfort during times of uncertainty. It also connects us to something greater than ourselves, reminding us that our lives are part of a larger plan.

In the Christian faith, purpose is often understood as fulfilling God's will and using our talents to serve His kingdom. This involves aligning our personal goals with God's purpose for us, living according to His teachings, and sharing His love with others. This alignment brings a sense of peace and fulfillment as we know that we are living in accordance with God's plan for our lives.

However, living a life of purpose according to faith is not without its challenges. It requires us to trust in God's timing, even when it doesn't align with our own. It also means being willing to surrender our own desires and ambitions in order to serve a higher purpose. This can be difficult, especially in a world that often values success and achievement over service and humility. It also requires us to trust that God's plan for us is better and more purposeful than our own. But that means taking the time to truly get to know God. On my journey, I struggled with this. I couldn't connect the dots.

I would pray to understand God's purpose for me, but I always seemed to fall short. The truth is the only wat to know God's plan is for you is to know God. There's no big formula – just get to know him. Pray.

One of the most powerful aspects of faith is its ability to provide hope and resilience in the face of adversity. When we encounter challenges, setbacks, or loss, our faith can anchor us, reminding us that there is a greater purpose behind our struggles. This perspective allows us to endure hardship with grace and to see our trials as opportunities for growth and spiritual development.

God and Purpose: Are They in Sync?

"My life is worth nothing unless I use it for doing the work assigned to me by the Lord Jesus—the work of telling others the Good News about God's wonderful kindness and love."
—*Acts 20:24 (NIV)*

If we believe that we are children of God, then our purpose is to live a life that glorifies Him. This means using our talents, experiences, and passions to serve others and spread His message of love and hope. For a long time, I struggled to understand my purpose because I was looking for something outside of myself. But the truth is, God has already given us everything we need to fulfill our purpose. It's up to us to recognize and use those gifts in a way that honors Him.

Living a life of purpose means aligning your personal goals with God's purpose for you. This doesn't mean you have to become a missionary or a preacher, but it does mean that your actions and decisions should reflect your faith and commitment to serving others. When you align your purpose with God's purpose, you'll find that your life takes on a new level of meaning and fulfillment.

For me, this alignment came when I started sharing my testimony and using my story to help others. I realized that my purpose wasn't just about overcoming my own baggage; it was about helping others do the same. By speaking and writing about my experiences, I could offer hope and guidance to those who were struggling just as I had. This is how I live my purpose in sync with God's plan for me.

But this alignment is not always easy to maintain. There are times when our personal desires conflict with what we believe is God's will for our lives. In these moments, it's important to seek guidance through prayer, reflection, and counsel from trusted spiritual advisors. It's also important to remember that God's plan may not always be clear to us in the moment, but we can trust that He is guiding us toward a greater purpose.

One of the challenges of aligning our purpose with God's purpose is the need to let go of control. As human beings, we often want to dictate the terms of our lives, setting specific goals and expectations for how things should unfold. But living a life of purpose according to faith requires us to surrender our need for control and trust that God's plan is better than anything we could devise on our own. This surrender is an act of faith and humility, and it allows us to live with greater peace and joy.

Another challenge is staying focused on God's purpose in a world that is constantly pulling us in different directions. We live in a society that often prioritizes success, wealth, and status over service, humility, and faithfulness. It can be difficult to stay true to our purpose when we are surrounded by messages that encourage us to pursue material gain or personal glory. This is why it's so important to regularly reconnect with God through prayer, worship, and spiritual practices that keep us grounded in our faith.

Purposeful Quotes to Live By

- *"The purpose of life is a life of purpose."* — Robert Byrne

- *"Our prime purpose in life is to help others, and if you can't help them, at least don't hurt them."* — Dalai Lama

- *"The meaning of life is to find your gift. The purpose of life is to give it away."* — Pablo Picasso

- *"The purpose of life is to believe, to hope, and to strive."* — Indira Gandhi

- *"The Lord will fulfill his purpose for me; your steadfast love, O Lord, endures forever."* — Psalm 138:8 (NIV)

- *"There is no failure except failure to serve one's purpose."* — Henry Ford

- *"When you're surrounded by people who share a passionate commitment around a common purpose, anything is possible."* — Howard Schultz, Starbucks

- *"Great things never come from comfortable zones"* – unknown

- *"You are never too old to set another goal or to dream a new dream"* – C.S. Lewis (my favorite one)

- *"All our dreams can come true, if we have the courage to pursue them"* – Walt Disney

- *"Give light and people will find the way"* – Ella Baker (my 2nd favorite one)

These quotes serve as reminders of the importance of living a life of purpose. Reflect on how these words resonate with your own experiences and aspirations. How can you incorporate the wisdom in these quotes into your daily life?

The Evolving Nature of Purpose

Purpose is not a static concept; it evolves as we grow and change. What you define as your purpose at one stage of your life may shift as you gain new experiences, insights, and perspectives. This evolution is a natural part of the journey, and it's important to remain open to the ways in which your purpose may expand or transform over time.

For example, your purpose in your twenties may be focused on building a career and establishing yourself professionally. As you move into your thirties or forties, your purpose may shift toward starting a family or giving back to your community. In your later years, your purpose may center around mentoring others or leaving a legacy. Each stage of life brings new opportunities to live your purpose in different ways.

This evolving nature of purpose requires flexibility and a willingness to adapt. It's important to regularly reassess your purpose and ensure that it still aligns with your values, passions, and goals. If you find that your purpose no longer resonates with you, it may be time to explore new directions and opportunities.

The key is to stay true to the core principles that define your purpose, even as the specifics of how you live that purpose may change. These core principles—such as serving others, living according to your values, and using your talents for good—provide a foundation that remains constant even as your purpose evolves.

The Role of Community in Living Your Purpose

Living a life of purpose is not something you do in isolation; it's deeply connected to the relationships and communities you are a part of. Community plays a vital role in helping you discover, live, and sustain your purpose. It provides support, accountability, and encouragement, as well as opportunities to serve and make a difference in the lives of others.

Being part of a community allows you to share your purpose with others and be inspired by their journeys as well. It fosters a sense of belonging and connection, reminding you that you are not alone in your quest to live a meaningful life. Whether trough a faith community, a professional network or a group of like-minded individuals, being connected to others who share your values and goals can greatly enhance your ability to live out your purpose.

I have expanded on the importance of community under Socially and Recreational Self-Aware, discussing how it plays a critical role in overcoming emotional baggage. Surrounding yourself with the people who encourage growth and share similar values can be a powerful strategy in your personal development and healing journey

One of the most powerful aspects of community is its ability to amplify your impact. When you join forces with others who are passionate about the same causes or goals, you can achieve far more than you could on your own. This collective effort creates a ripple effect, where each person's contribution is magnified, and the overall impact is greater than the sum of its parts.

However, it's important to choose your community wisely. Surround yourself with people who support your purpose and encourage your growth. Seek out those who challenge you to be better, who hold you accountable to your goals, and who celebrate your successes with you. These are the people who will help you stay focused on your purpose, even when the path is difficult.

Overcoming Challenges to Stay Aligned with Your Purpose

Living a life of purpose is deeply fulfilling, but it's not without its challenges. There will be times when you feel lost, discouraged, or tempted to give up. These challenges are a natural part of the journey, and it's important to be prepared for them.

One of the biggest challenges is staying true to your purpose in the face of external pressures. Society often pushes us to conform to certain standards of success or happiness that may not align with our true purpose. It can be difficult to resist these pressures, especially when they come from people we care about or from cultural norms that are deeply ingrained. I'm going to offer an example that might be considered controversial. When Hillary Clinton ran for president, here campaign chose the Jacob Javits Center in NYC for their election night event, a venue known for its glass ceiling. Hillary aimed to break the glass ceiling at the highest level. However, I take a different perspective on the concept of the glass ceiling.

I believe that the idea of a glass ceiling is a limiting belief that society has created as women have progressed throughout history. If you believe there's a glass ceiling, then you're likely focusing on what you can't do rather than what you can achieve. Many remarkable women have achieved greatness not because they were trying to break the glass ceiling, but because they pursued their goals with passion and purpose, regardless of any perceived barriers.

For instance, Jeanette Ranking became the first woman elected to the U.S. Congress in 1916, and Frances Perkins was appointed to the presidential cabinet in 1932 by Franklin Roosevelt. In 1981, Sandra Day O'Connor became the first female Supreme Court justice appointed by Ronald Reagan, and Aretha Franklin was the first woman and woman of color, inducted into the Rock & Roll Hall of Fame in 1987. These women, and many others, didn't focus on breaking a glass ceiling – they focused on their dedication to their work and their purpose of life.

When we think of incredible women we know or admire, is it because they broke through a glass ceiling, or because they were committed to hard work and pursuing their purpose? Perhaps Hillary Clinton didn't become the first female president because too much attention was placed glass ceiling itself, rather than on the larger vision.

Another challenge is dealing with setbacks and failures. When things don't go as planned, it's easy to question your purpose and wonder if you're on the right path. These moments of doubt can be paralyzing, but they are also opportunities for growth. By staying committed to your purpose and learning from your experiences, you can emerge stronger and more focused on your goals.

Maintaining balance is another challenge. It's important to pursue your purpose with passion and determination, but it's equally important to take care of yourself and avoid burnout. This means setting boundaries, taking time to rest and recharge, and seeking support when needed. Remember, your purpose is not a sprint; it's a marathon, and it's essential to pace yourself and take care of your well-being along the way.

Finally, it's important to remain adaptable and open to change. As you pursue your purpose, you may encounter new opportunities, challenges, and insights that require you to adjust your path. Being flexible and willing to evolve will help you stay aligned with your purpose, even as the circumstances of your life change.

Reflection and Application: Living Your Purpose Daily

Living a life of purpose is not just about the big moments; it's about the daily choices and actions that align with your purpose. This means being intentional in how you spend your time, energy, and resources, and ensuring that your decisions reflect your values and goals.

One practical way to live your purpose daily is to start each day with intention. Take a few moments in the morning to reflect on your purpose and set an intention for how you will live that purpose throughout the day. Don't turn a molehill into a mountain – keep things in perspective. This could be as simple as committing to act with kindness, to seek opportunities to serve others, or to focus on a specific goal that aligns with your purpose.

Another way to live your purpose daily is to create habits and routines that support your goals. These could include practices like journaling, meditation, or regular check ins with a mentor or accountability partner. By building these habits into your daily life, you create a structure that helps you stay focused on your purpose and make progress toward your goals.

It's also important to regularly reflect on your actions and decisions to ensure they are in alignment with your purpose. This could be done through a daily or weekly review, where you assess how you've spent your time and whether your choices have supported your long-term goals. This reflection allows you to adjust as needed and ensures that you are staying true to your purpose.

Finally, remember to celebrate your successes, both big and small. Living a life of purpose is a journey, and it's important to acknowledge and celebrate the progress you've made. This not only boosts your motivation but also reinforces the positive impact you are making in the world. Celebrating my successes was once very hard for me, because I was very hard on myself. People often gave me more credit than I thought I deserved. To change this, I decided to create a success book. Going back 30 years, this book contains every certificate I ever earned, every competition I got a ribbon for, every letter of recommendation that was ever written for me, every business award I ever received, every letter of accommodation or military promotion I ever received and every educational degree I have ever earned. Doing this helped me get out of my head. In this book I created a list called Never did I think:

Never Did I Think

Never did I think I could overcome my reading issues that plagued me when I was young.
Never did I think I would be on stage with Johnny Cash giving my testimony on live TV.
Never did I think I would serve in the U.S Army, be all I can be and live in a different country.
Never did I think I could earn a Bachelor of Science Degree in Organizational Behavior.
Never in a million years did I think I could earn a master's degree in executive leadership.
Never did I think I could hold a job for more than two years.

Never did I think I could work in the same industry
for over 10 years.
Never did I think I would have two certifications in Coaching
and Public Speaking
Never did I think my family could actually love each other;
we do now.
Never did I think I would be an Author. Here it is.
Never did I think I would be living a purpose driven life.
Never did I think I would, despite it all, raise an amazingly
successful daughter.

But now I know that God loved me through it all!

Never did I think......... but oh boy, I DID

I haven't gone back to my success book in a long time, which could be considered a good thing. Life isn't over, and I am sure I would have more successes to add. If you had to create a success book, what would it look like? What would the title be? Even if you feel you have only one success, create the book. More successes will follow.

The Lifelong Journey of Purpose

Living a life of purpose is one of the most rewarding and fulfilling journeys you can embark on. It requires courage, commitment, and a willingness to continually grow and evolve. But the rewards are immense—a life of meaning, fulfillment, and impact.

As you move forward on this journey, remember that your purpose is not a destination; it's a lifelong process of discovery and growth. There will be challenges along the way, but by staying true to your values, embracing your passions, and aligning your actions with your purpose, you can overcome these challenges and live a life of significance.

You have everything you need to live your purpose. The talents, strengths, and experiences that make you unique are the very tools that will help you fulfill your purpose. By using these gifts in service of others, you not only make a positive impact on the world but also find the deep fulfillment that comes from living a life aligned with your true self.

As you continue on this journey, remember to stay connected to your faith, seek support from your community, and remain open to the ways in which your purpose may evolve. By doing so, you will not only live a life of purpose but also inspire others to do the same.

Chapter 9

Living Baggage Free

"Life truly is a journey, and the less baggage we carry,
the easier the ride."
—*Wally Amos*

Congratulations on reaching this point in your journey. You've done the hard work, but remember, the work of overcoming emotional baggage is never truly done. You might be thinking, "Wait, there's more?" Yes, there is more. Living baggage free isn't a one time achievement; it's an ongoing process, much like maintaining any valuable relationship in life. Whether it's personal growth, a career, or your mental health, the key is retention and growth. You are the customer of your own life, and it's essential to continually nurture yourself just as you would a long-term client in business.

When conducting leadership training, I often talk about how we are all born leaders. However, as we grow we develop our leadership skills throughout our lives determines how well we lead ourselves and others. The reference to seeing yourself as the CEO of the company of you works well here. Remember my company name is - Fausta Phelan Inc. If I want to grow this company to achieve success, I need to grow from the inside out, building a strong foundation that I can rely on. My product is living my purpose, and my compensation and true measure of success is the rewarding feeling I will have by creating a positive impact in a person's world even if it is one person at a time; all for the glory of God. My slogan will be what it was in my military unit – Always out Front, reminding me to always look forward, even when the past intersects with your present. Always out Front is the positive mindset that will take me to the next level of my purpose.

The analogy of viewing oneself as a company can be a powerful tool for personal growth. Just like any successful business, personal development requires regular audits, adjustments, and reinvestments. What is your mission statement? What are your core values? These are the guiding principles that will help you stay aligned with your goals, especially when life's challenges arise.

One of the most valuable lessons I've learned is that emotional baggage is like an old business debt. You might ignore it for a while, but eventually, it will come due—with interest. If you want to keep your personal "company" thriving, you have to address these debts head on. Whether through therapy, self-reflection, or spiritual growth, acknowledging and dealing with your past is essential to living a baggage free life.

Reflect on your own journey: How have you managed the intersection of your past and present? What strategies have helped you reconcile these moments?

Embrace the Empowerment

Initially, enjoy the empowerment that comes with reconciling your baggage. Celebrate yourself and take pride in what you've accomplished. I remember that feeling well. I felt lighter, with a fresh outlook on life, and a sense of direction that motivated me to create a better plan for my future. However, I soon realized that while the feeling of empowerment was powerful, it wasn't enough to sustain lasting change. Like the initial excitement of a new relationship, feelings alone aren't enough to build a solid foundation. Without nurturing those feelings and turning them into intentional habits, they won't last.

When I started my journey, I had different expectations. I thought I was finally "cured," but I didn't realize that years of unreconciled baggage meant there were layers of it still needing to be addressed. I learned that reconciling emotional baggage could feel light at times and heavy at others. My advice is to continue growing, reconciling one layer at a time. Remember, this is a journey, not a destination. Life is a continuous process of growth, whether you have baggage or not.

Empowerment is not just about feeling good; it's about creating a solid foundation that can withstand the tests of time and adversity. This foundation is built on self-awareness, resilience, and the willingness to confront and learn from past experiences. Empowerment also involves acknowledging your strengths and using them to navigate through life's challenges.

One key aspect of maintaining empowerment is the concept of self-compassion. Too often, we are our own harshest critics, especially when we stumble. Learning to be kind to yourself, to treat yourself with the same understanding and patience you would offer a dear friend, is crucial. Self-compassion does not mean avoiding responsibility; rather, it means acknowledging your humanity and allowing yourself to grow from every experience.

> **Reflect on your strengths: How have they helped you overcome obstacles in your life? How can you continue to build on these strengths moving forward?**

How do you handle the ups and downs in your journey of growth? What practices help you maintain your progress even when new challenges arise?

Consider incorporating daily or weekly practices that reinforce this empowerment. Journaling about your progress, setting new goals, and celebrating small victories can keep you focused and motivated. Remember, empowerment is a state of being that requires ongoing cultivation.

Living Baggage Free: A Continuous Journey

Living baggage free means being prepared for when the initial triumph wears off and the daily grind and stresses of life begin. It's essentially a maintenance program for life that allows you to continue cultivating healthy relationships, maintaining a healthy state of well being, and setting your life up to leave a legacy—a legacy that goes beyond just yourself—perhaps in my case, beyond Fausta Phelan Inc.

One of the greatest things we can do with our reconciled emotional baggage is to help others overcome theirs. We know the signs; we've lived through it ourselves. If you are growing the leader within you, you'll understand that the best leaders grow other leaders. So don't keep your triumph to yourself. Continue living triumphantly by helping others. One way to do this is to be a role model. Shifting your focus from yourself to others can sustain your life of living baggage free. As you continue to grow, people will notice the difference in you and may even be inspired by you.

Living a baggage-free life isn't just about personal freedom; it also allows you to contribute more fully to the well-being of others. When you shift from self-focus to focusing on others, you create a ripple effect that can positively impact your community and beyond. By becoming a role model, you not only reinforce your own growth but also pave the way for others to embark on their journeys. If you have children, don't be surprised if they become your role models at times. Children have a way of seeing things simply, which can be incredibly helpful for adults who often view life through a more complicated lens. I had this experience with my daughter when she was just 16 years old – it was a real jolt to my heart. Once I got over the shock, I realized she was right. I needed to be more like her.

Brittney, my daughter is the most driven and disciplined person I know. While I have taught her residence, she took those strengths and truly made them her own, living her dream with incredible determination. She inspires me every day. She believes in me; many times more than I believe in myself. Now, we are each other's role models

One of the best ways to reinforce your progress and ensure you continue to live baggage free is by teaching others what you've learned. Whether it's mentoring a younger person, volunteering, or simply being a friend who listens and offers advice, sharing your experiences helps solidify your own understanding and keeps you accountable. It's said that the best way to learn is to teach, and this certainly applies to personal growth.

Consider the impact you could have on others: How can you use your experiences to support and inspire those around you?

Who in your life could benefit from your guidance and wisdom?

> Think about the people in your life who have inspired you: What qualities do they possess that you admire? How can you embody these qualities in your interactions with others?

Know That You Can Make a Difference

It's easy to let limiting beliefs creep in and convince you that you have nothing to offer beyond your own personal growth. During my journey, I knew I had talents and big dreams, but the child in me often questioned, "How can I, one person, make a difference?" These doubts stem from the shared coping skill tied to our be my baggage? Notice how these questions often begin with "how can I" or "what if." Instead of focusing on the doubt, rephrase the question to "How can I use what I've learned to effect positive change?"

Reframing your internal dialogue from doubt to intention is a powerful first step in believing you can make a difference. It's not about eliminating the questions but turning them into positive affirmations. For example, "I can make a difference—if I choose to put my mind, heart, and soul into the cause and take action." Intentional words like "can" and "choose" are powerful because they shift your mindset from passivity to action. If you want to affirm what you "can do" level up and use the word "will". I took a personality test that measures levels f your Can-do vs WILL-DO. There is a difference. Can-do means you have the ability to do something but may or may not do it. WILL-DO is a commitment statement. You affirmed that "it" will be done.

When we think of making a difference, we often imagine grand gestures or significant changes. However, making a difference doesn't always mean changing the world overnight. It can start with small, consistent actions that build up over time. Whether it's offering a listening ear to someone in need, volunteering your time, or simply being kind to those around you, these small acts can have a profound impact.

For instance, I remember a time when I doubted my ability to make a meaningful impact. I felt that my contributions were too small to matter. But then a friend reminded me of the story of the starfish. In the story, a boy is throwing starfish back into the ocean one by one. A man approaches him and says, "There are thousands of starfish stranded on the beach. You can't possibly make a difference." The boy picks up another starfish, throws it into the ocean, and says, "I made a difference for that one."

This story resonates deeply with me because it illustrates the power of small, intentional actions. Each starfish saved represents a life touched, a difference made. It's a reminder that every effort counts, no matter how small it may seem.

> **Take a moment to rephrase a doubt or fear you have into a positive statement of intention. How does this new perspective feel?**

> **Reflect on the small ways you can make a difference in your daily life: What simple actions can you take today to contribute to the well-being of others?**

Reframing your internal dialogue and focusing on the positive impact you can have—no matter the scale—can transform your approach to life. It's about shifting from a mindset of scarcity to one of abundance, recognizing that you have more to offer than you may have realized.

Living an Intentional Life

To live a baggage free life, living intentionally is essential. Intentional living isn't the same as having good intentions, which often lack follow through. It's about turning thought into action.

In John Maxwell's book *Intentional Living*, he distinguishes between wishing for things to change and taking the necessary actions to make those changes a reality. This shift from desire to deed is the essence of living intentionally. When I was burdened by unreconciled baggage, I spent a lot of time wishing, dreaming, and hoping, but I wasn't doing. It wasn't until I began to live intentionally that I saw real change. If you find yourself stuck in your baggage, start by writing down your thoughts in terms of action, not desire. This shift can be a game changer.

Intentional living embraces only the things that add to your life's mission, your significance on earth, and the legacy you will leave behind. The more you live intentionally, the more you attract like-minded people into your life. Start small with your actions and don't overwhelm yourself with high expectations. Each accomplishment is a step toward your overall mission.

One thing I've learned is the power of saying "no" to what doesn't serve my mission. Early in my journey, I found myself overwhelmed by obligations and commitments that drained my energy and time. I realized that by saying "yes" to everything, I was saying "no" to the things that truly mattered. Intentional living means being selective about where you invest your time and energy, ensuring that your actions align with your goals and values.

For example, I once took on a project that, in hindsight, did not align with my personal or professional goals. I was drawn to it out of a sense of obligation and the fear of disappointing others. The project consumed a significant amount of my time and energy, leaving me feeling depleted and unfulfilled. It was a hard lesson, but it taught me the importance of setting boundaries and prioritizing what truly matters.

> **Reflect on your long-term goals: What are they, and how can you break them down into smaller, actionable steps that you can start today?**

Living intentionally doesn't mean you'll avoid all baggage in the future, but it does mean you'll be better equipped to handle it. Over time, you'll find that discomfort becomes less intimidating, and you'll view challenges as opportunities for growth. Eventually, the fear of discomfort fades away, revealing that it was just a limiting belief created by your baggage to protect yourself. But you don't need that protection anymore.

This realization came to me during a particularly challenging period when I was transitioning between careers. The fear of failure and the discomfort of the unknown were overwhelming. Get comfortable with being uncomfortable. When you're too comfortable, you stop growing, so embracing discomfort is always a step in the right direction. By focusing on living intentionally - getting comfortable with discomfort, setting clear goals, taking small steps, surrounding myself with supportive people – I was able to move through the discomfort and come out stronger on the other side.

> How has your mindset shifted throughout this journey?
> What limiting beliefs are you ready to let go of?

Changing Your Mindset

In my journey to unload all my dysfunctional baggage, I learned about the power of mindset from Carol S. Dweck's book *Mindset: The New Psychology of Success*. She explains that we have the power to change our world by choosing between a growth mindset and a fixed mindset. If you're suffering from emotional baggage, you may be living in a fixed mindset where you believe your traits and abilities are static and cannot change.

But choosing a mindset is a choice. A growth mindset encourages us to embrace challenges, learn from feedback, and persist despite obstacles. It allows us to see our journey as a path to mastery rather than a series of failures. This mindset shift was a turning point for me. I began to see setbacks not as failures but as opportunities to learn and grow.

For example, when I first started speaking publicly about my experiences with emotional baggage, I was terrified. My fixed mindset told me that I wasn't a good speaker, that I would fail, and that people wouldn't be interested in what I had to say. But I pushed through those fears, adopting a growth mindset that focused on improving with each speaking engagement. Over time, I became more confident, and what once felt impossible became something I genuinely enjoyed. I also change my focus to the audience instead of myself. Afterall the audience is there to gain something from you.

> Reflect on your current mindset: Do you tend to see challenges as insurmountable obstacles or as opportunities to learn and grow? How can you begin to shift towards a growth mindset in areas where you feel stuck?

The Power of Reframing

One of the most powerful tools in changing your mindset is the practice of reframing. Reframing involves taking a negative thought or situation and looking at it from a different, more positive perspective. It's about changing the narrative you tell yourself, which in turn changes your experience of reality.

For example, instead of thinking, "I'm not good enough to achieve this goal," you can reframe it to, "I'm capable of learning and growing, and each step I take brings me closer to my goal." This simple shift in language can have a profound impact on your confidence and motivation.

Reframing isn't about ignoring the challenges or pretending that everything is perfect. It's about acknowledging the difficulties and choosing to focus on the possibilities rather than the limitations. It's a way to take control of your narrative and direct it toward growth and positivity.

Reframing has been a powerful tool in my own journey. There was a time when I viewed certain challenges in my life as insurmountable, as signs that I wasn't capable or worthy of success. But through the practice of reframing, I began to see these challenges as opportunities to develop resilience, to prove to myself that I could handle whatever came my way. This shift in perspective didn't just change how I approached challenges; it changed how I viewed myself and my capabilities.

> **Take a moment to identify a negative thought you've had recently. How can you reframe this thought into something more positive and empowering?**

How can you make reframing a regular practice in your life? What situations or thoughts could benefit from a new perspective?

Choosing the Right People Along the Way

Your journey to living a baggage free life cannot be done alone. As much as those of us with emotional baggage prefer to go it alone—DON'T! Fight that urges. One of the most critical decisions you will make is choosing the right people to support you on this journey.

Consider these questions to help you identify the right people to surround yourself with:

- Who in your life currently offers you a baseline of wisdom?
- Who in your life has inspired you or others?
- Who challenges you to think and look at things from different perspectives?

- Who are your cheerleaders of dreams and believe all things are possible if you do the work to get there?

- Who in your life cares enough to constructively rebuke you and hold you accountable?

- Who sees your failures as opportunities to grow?

- Who encourages you when you are discouraged by your burdens?

- Who reminds you to laugh and have good, clean fun?

- Who inspires you to faithfully seek God?

Choosing the right person to walk with you on this journey can make all the difference. It's about finding people who reflect the values and aspirations you want to cultivate in yourself.

Building a strong support system is crucial to maintaining your progress. These are the people who will hold you accountable, offer guidance, and celebrate your victories with you. They are the ones who will remind you of your worth when you forget it yourself.

One important lesson I've learned is that not everyone in your life will understand your journey – and that's okay. Don't take it personally. More often than not, it's not about you. My daughter struggled with other people's opinions, and to help her overcome this, I would always ask, "Why are you choosing to carry their baggage? When you do, their baggage mixes with yours, making the load unnecessarily heavy." Instead, I encouraged her to surround herself with people who understand her, see her potential and are committed to helping her grow.

This may mean letting go of relationships that no longer serve you or deepening the ones that do. In Brittney's case, she eventually had to let go of a relationship she once admired. You can see the weight lifted from her shoulders now. If you're in a situation where you can't change your surroundings, just yet, try expanding your circle of influence and surround yourself with people who are rooting for you. That's what I did as a child, and it certainly paid off in many ways.

> **Reflect on the people in your life: Who fits these criteria? How can you cultivate and strengthen these relationships?**

One of the most profound experiences I had in this regard was realizing the power of mentorship. Throughout my journey, I sought out mentors who had walked similar paths, who had the wisdom and experience to guide me through my own struggles. These mentors didn't just offer advice—they offered hope. They showed me that it was possible to overcome my baggage and live a life of purpose and fulfillment.

Who in your life do you feel truly supports your growth and well-being? How can you invest more in these relationships?

"When the student is ready, the teacher will appear." This statement from Jim Ryan's *Simple Happiness* perfectly captures what happens when you decide to live a baggage free life. Whether you believe in cosmic energy or have faith in Jesus Christ, the message is the same—all things are possible if you believe they are.

Living baggage free is not about perfection; it's about progress. It's about recognizing that while the journey may be challenging, it is also incredibly rewarding. Each step you take brings you closer to a life of freedom, peace, and fulfillment.

As you move forward, remember that this journey is ongoing. There will be days when you feel like you're backsliding or when old habits and thoughts resurface. This is normal. What's important is how you respond to these moments. Instead of giving up, use these experiences as opportunities to learn and grow.

Finally, know that living a baggage free life is one of the greatest gifts you can give to yourself and to those around you. By freeing yourself from the weight of the past, you open yourself up to new possibilities and experiences. You become a beacon of hope and inspiration to others who are on their own journeys.

> What does living a baggage free life mean to you? How can you continue to cultivate this way of living in your daily life?

The Journey Continues

As we conclude this chapter, take a moment to reflect on the progress you've made. You've come a long way in your journey to living baggage free, but remember, the journey doesn't end here. It's a continuous process of growth, learning, and self-discovery. If it feels like I'm repeating this message, it is because I am – that's how important it is. When life feels like it's repeating itself, come back to these words and remember that it's simply a lesson, guiding you to take on more step forward.

One of the key takeaways from this chapter is that living a baggage free life requires ongoing effort and intentionality. It's not something that happens overnight, and it's not something that you achieve once and then forget about. Just as you would regularly service a car to keep it running smoothly, you need to regularly check in with yourself to ensure that you're living in alignment with your values and goals.

This means continually reassessing your mindset, your relationships, and your actions. Are you still holding onto beliefs that no longer serve you? Are there people in your life who are draining your energy rather than supporting your growth? Are your daily actions moving you closer to your goals, or are they keeping you stuck?

These are the kinds of questions you should ask yourself regularly as you continue on your journey. Remember, the goal is not to be perfect but to be constantly evolving, learning, and growing.

As you continue your journey, I encourage you to take steps that reflect your heart's desire for healing and reconciliation. Close your eyes, find you peace and listen to God. He may be speaking to you. Healing takes time, and each step – no matter how small – moves you closer to freedom from the burdens of the past. Remember, forgiveness and growth don't happen overnight, but with each act of grace and openness, you'll find yourself becoming light, stronger and more at peace.

You are not alone on this path. Many have walked it before, including myself , and others will walk it after you. By sharing your story and embracing the lessons you've learned, you can break the cycle of pain and create a legacy of love and understanding for future generations.

In the next chapter, we'll dive deeper into how to sustain this healing and continue building a life rich in purpose, peace and joy that comes from living with a heart unburdened by the past.

Chapter 10

A Letter to You – Embracing Family Healing

"Get rid of all bitterness, rage and anger, brawling and slander, along with every form of malice. Be kind and compassionate to one another, forgiving each other, just as Christ God forgave you."
– Ephesians 4:31 (NIV)

Dear Reader,

I want to take a moment to speak directly to you—not just as an author but as someone who has walked the rocky path of reconciliation and healing. I've been where you are, carrying the weight of emotional baggage that at times felt impossible to bear. But I'm here to tell you that healing is possible. It's within reach, and it begins with a single courageous step.

Living baggage free has brought me more than I ever imagined. I won't pretend that emotional baggage no longer exists in my life—it does for all of us. But now it's like a scar on my skin; a reminder of what I've been through but also proof that I've healed. The past no longer defines me; instead, it teaches me, and it can teach you too.

For the longest time, the biggest scar I carried was the loss of my family. By the time I was 14, I had mentally divorced myself from them. The pain was too great, and it was easier to resent them than to confront the hurt. I went to college with one goal: to never look back. I had no use for them, much like my father had no use for us. And so, I carried that pain with me through most of my adult life, keeping my distance, believing that separation was the only way to protect myself.

But life has a way of surprising us, doesn't it? Never in my wildest dreams did I think that my siblings and I would reconnect as a family unit. Too much time had passed; too much pain had accumulated. But sometimes healing starts in the most unexpected ways. For me, it began at a wedding—my niece's wedding. It was the first time in nearly 20 years that we were all in the same place. The air was thick with unease but also with something else: hope. We sat together, reminisced, and slowly the layers of anger and resentment began to peel away. It wasn't immediate, but it was a start.

I want to encourage you to take a moment and think about your own family. Are there relationships that need mending? Hurts that need healing. I know it's hard, and I know it's scary. But believe me when I say the first step is the hardest, but also the most rewarding. Start small. A conversation, a letter, even a prayer. Acknowledge the past but don't let it hold you captive.

For years, I struggled with forgiveness—both of myself and my family. But my journey towards healing truly began when I allowed God to enter the process. There were nights when I sat alone, Bible in hand, asking for the strength to forgive. Philippians 4:13 became my lifeline: "I can do all things through Christ who strengthens me." I learned that forgiveness is not about forgetting or excusing what happened; it's about freeing yourself from the chains of resentment and pain.

If faith is a part of your life, I encourage you to lean into it during this time. Let God be your guide as you navigate the complex emotions of reconciliation. Pray for the strength to forgive, the courage to reach out, and the wisdom to know when and how to move forward. And if faith isn't part of your journey, I still urge you to find that inner strength—whether it's through meditation, reflection, or simply the act of letting go.

Time, I've learned, is both a healer and a barrier. It allows us to grow and gain perspective, but it can also harden our hearts if we're not careful. I often wonder what would have happened if my family and I had tried to reconcile sooner. But I also recognize that the years apart gave us the space we needed to confront our demons independently. It made our reunion that much more meaningful.

Reflect on the role time has played in your relationships. Has it been a friend or a foe? Remember, it's never too late to heal. The passage of time can create distance, but it can also offer the perspective needed to approach old wounds with new eyes. Don't let too much time slip away before you take that first step toward healing.

One of the most beautiful outcomes of my family's reconciliation is the impact it has had on the next generation. My daughter, who witnessed the fractured relationships within our family, now sees the possibility of healing and forgiveness. This has taught her the importance of resolving conflicts and not letting past hurts dictate the future. And that, my friend, is a gift beyond measure.

Your healing journey isn't just about you—it's about the generations that follow. The steps you take today can break cycles of pain and create a legacy of love and understanding. Imagine the impact your healing could have on your children, grandchildren, and beyond. That's the power you hold in your hands.

As I write this, I am filled with gratitude for the unexpected gift of family reconciliation. My siblings and I are now in our 60s, and we are so thankful that we found our way back to each other. It wasn't easy, and it didn't happen overnight, but with God's help, it happened. And it can happen for you too.

What brought us together was one common denominator— God. This was the last thing I ever expected out of my siblings, but what it taught me is that in His own time, God will do the work that is needed. All of my siblings are now free from the lifestyle and addiction of drugs and alcohol. Each one, at very different times in their lives, faced their rock bottom and slowly began the journey of recovery. It took some longer than others, but in the end, and without leaning on each other, they made that recovery journey. It is not just me living baggage free, but my siblings too. We are all grateful to God for our healing and our reconciliation.

I urge you to take that first step today. Reach out to the family member you've been avoiding. Open your heart to the possibility of forgiveness and healing. Remember, the journey of healing is not a sprint—it's a marathon. But every small step you take brings you closer to the freedom of living baggage free. You have the power to change your family's story. Don't let that opportunity slip away.

As you take these steps, know that there are resources available to help you along the way. Whether it's seeking professional counseling, joining a support group, or engaging with a coach who can guide you through the process, don't hesitate to reach out for help. Healing is not something you have to do alone.

Thank you for allowing me to share my story with you. I hope it has given you the courage to face your own challenges, the hope to believe in the possibility of healing, and the strength to take that first step toward reconciliation. You are not alone on this journey, and I am cheering you on every step of the way.

With love and encouragement,
Fausta

About the Author

Fausta Phelan is a passionate advocate for personal growth, leadership, and empowerment. With years of experience in guiding individuals and teams toward achieving their highest potential, Fausta Phelan has dedicated her life to helping others break free from the emotional baggage that holds them back. Her unique approach to coaching and leadership is grounded in her deep understanding of human behavior, combined with her commitment to fostering environments where individuals can thrive.

As the founder of FCP Leadership Services, Inc., Fausta has developed programs that empower individuals to lead with purpose and authenticity. Her work emphasizes the importance of self-awareness, resilience, and the power of choice in navigating life's challenges. Through her coaching, workshops, and speaking engagements, Fausta has inspired countless individuals to take control of their lives, shed their past burdens, and step confidently into their future.

Fausta Phelan's own journey of overcoming personal challenges and emotional baggage has equipped her with the insights and tools to guide others on a similar path. Her mission is to help people not just survive but truly thrive by Living Baggage Free from the weight of the past and empowered to embrace the present and future with strength and purpose.

When she's not coaching or speaking, Fausta enjoys exploring new places, playing golf, hiking, and spending time with her daughter both stateside and abroad. Fausta also finds fulfillment in serving on the production team at her church, where she enjoys growing in her faith.

She believes in the power of community and is committed to making a positive impact on the world, one person at a time.

Transform Your Life with Fausta Phelan

Fausta Phelan offers a range of services designed to help you unlock your potential, overcome emotional barriers, and lead a life of purpose.

Personal Growth Coaching: Work with Fausta to break free from the emotional baggage that holds you back, set and achieve meaningful goals, and cultivate a resilient mindset.

Leadership Development: Learn to lead with authenticity, enhance your communication skills, and build a cohesive, high performing team that thrives on collaboration.

Resilience Training: Develop the mental and emotional strength needed to face life's challenges. Fausta's training includes practical stress management techniques and empowerment workshops designed to help you take control of your future.

Customized Workshops & Speaking Engagements: Fausta offers tailored training programs and inspirational speaking engagements that resonate with your audience and drive real change.

FCP Leadership Services Programs: Discover purpose driven leadership and embark on a journey of self-discovery to achieve balance and fulfillment in your personal, professional, and spiritual life.

Fausta brings years of experience and proven expertise in personal development and leadership. Her personalized approach ensures that each session is tailored to your unique needs, leading to significant personal growth and lasting impact.

Take the First Step Towards Your Best Life!

Scan the code below to contact Fausta Phelan today to discover how her services can help you lead with purpose and transform your life.

Resources used for Living Baggage Free

Dale Carnegie, *How To Stop Worrying and Start Living,* Simon & Schuster, Inc., 1984

John C. Maxwell and Rob Hoskins, *Change Your World,* Maxwell Motivational, Inc. & AnimoCorvern, LLC., 2021

John C. Maxwell, *The 15 Invaluable Laws of Growth-10 Anniversary Edition,* Center Street, Inc. (div of Hachette Book Group, New York, NY 2022

Scott Moorehead and Ryan McCarty, *Build a Culture of Good,* Carmel of Good Inc., Carmel, IN 2017

Rick Warren, *A Purpose Driven Life,* Expanded Edition, Zondervan, Grand Rapids, MI, 2012

Kevin Cashman, *Leadership From The Inside Out,* Berrett-Koehler Publishers, Inc., San Francisco, CA, 2008

Clayton M. Christensen, *HBR'S 10 Must Reads-On Managing Yourself,* Harvard Business Review Press, Boston, MA, 2010

John C. Maxwell, *Put Your Dream To the Test,* Thomas Nelson Inc., Nashville, TN, 2011

David R Hawkins, M.D., Ph.D., *Letting Go, The Pathway to Surrender,* Hay House Inc., New York, NY, 2012

Tal Ben-Shahar, Ph.D., *Choose the Life You Want, The Mindful Way to Happiness,* The Experiment, LLC, New York, NY 2012

Robert S. McGee, *The Search for Significance,* Thomas Nelson, Inc., Nashville, TN, 2003

Jim Ryan, *Simple Happiness,* JoyRide Visions Publishing, Northport, NY, 2014

Carol S. Dweck, Ph.D., *Mindset, The New Psychology of Success-How We Can Learn to Fill Our Potential,* Ballantine Books (div of Penguin Random House, Inc)., New York, NY, 2016

John C. Maxwell, *How Successful People Think,* Center Street (div of Hachette Book Group), New York, NY, 2009

John C. Maxwell, *Intentional Living- Choosing A Life That Matters,* **Center Street (div of Hachette Book Group), New York, NY, 2015**

John C. Maxwell, *The Maxwell Leadership Bible, NIV,* **Thomas Nelson, Inc. Nashville, TN, 2018**

INTERNET RESOURCES

Reference: Divorce for Baby Boomers, Sharon Jayson, AARP, Sept 2023 - https://www.aarp.org/home-family/friends-family/info-2023/gray-divorce-trend.html

Reference: Divorce in America, David Epps, The Citizen, Nove 2021- https://thecitizen.com/2021/11/03/divorce-in-america/